ROOTED & GROUNDED

GROUNDED

GOING DEEPER INTO DISCIPLESHIP

CALVARY CASTLE ROCK

ILLUMIFY
MEDIA.COM

Published by
Illumify Media Global
www.IllumifyMedia.com
"Let's bring your book to life!"

Paperback ISBN: 978-1-970582-08-6

Cover design by Debbie Lewis

Printed in the United States of America

Dedicated to the glory of Jesus Christ to accomplish
His mandate to make disciples of all the nations for
the building up of His body, the church.

Contents

Introduction

Welcome! I am so grateful you have chosen to go deeper in your faith. We read in God's Word, "But as many as received Him, to them He gave the right to become children of God, to those who believe in His name" (John 1:12). When you received Jesus, you became a child of God. As a child of God, the next step is to grow in your faith and become godly men and women. This is discipleship.

Jesus, after His resurrection, gave His disciples instructions in Galilee saying to them, "Go therefore and make disciples of all the nations, baptizing them in the name of the Father and of the Son and of the Holy Spirit, teaching them to observe all things that I have commanded you; and lo, I am with you always, even to the end of the age" (Matthew 28:19–20).

Jesus spent three and a half years training His disciples, and now He is commanding them to disciple others. The word *disciple* is a Greek word, μαθητής, or *mathetes*, which means a learner, a pupil, one who takes up knowledge or beliefs from his teacher. Jesus said in Luke 6:40, "A disciple is not above his teacher, but everyone who is perfectly trained will be like his teacher."

To be a disciple of Jesus is to learn everything about Him and what He desires from us as His disciples—so we can be like Him. To become like Him is the process of sanctification. This book will serve as a tool to help you become a mature believer in Jesus, which will bring praise and glory to Him.

When Jesus was asked what the greatest commandment is, He replied, "You shall love the LORD your God with all your heart, with all your soul, and with all your mind" (Matthew 22:37).

He went on to say, "This is the first and greatest commandment. And the second is like it: 'You shall love your neighbor as yourself.' On these two commandments hang all the Law and the Prophets" (Matthew 22:38–40).

The first and greatest command is toward God: to love Him. The second greatest command is toward others: to love them.

The first book of the Rooted and Grounded series focuses on the command to love God. To love God, you must know Him. This book is entirely about knowing God so that you can love Him. The next book will focus on loving others, as you cannot love others until you first love God.

There are eight chapters in this book. However, you may decide to take a few weeks to go through each chapter. Allow time to ask questions or explore further. You and the person discipling you can choose a pace you are comfortable with.

The book's title, *Rooted and Grounded*, is derived from Jesus's Parable of the Sower in Matthew 13. In this parable, Jesus describes a Sower who scatters seeds that represent the Word of God. The seeds fall on four types of soil, with the fourth type being good soil, which produces a fruitful plant yielding a crop of a hundredfold, some sixty, and others thirty.

Another type of soil is the stony ground, and Jesus says, "But he who received the seed on stony places, this is he who hears the word and immediately receives it with joy; yet he has no root in himself but endures only for a while. For when tribulation or persecution arises because of the word, immediately he stumbles" (Matthew 13:20–21).

Thus, we can conclude that lacking a healthy root system will result in being unfruitful. Jesus said of the good ground, "But he who received seed on the good ground is he who hears the word and understands it, who indeed bears fruit and produces: some a hundredfold, some sixty, some thirty" (Matthew 13:23).

Hearing and understanding the Word refers to having a good, solid ground or foundation for developing a deep root system for your faith.

It is my prayer that this discipleship book will help you become rooted and grounded in the Word of God so that you may bear much fruit for the Kingdom of God, and at the end of your life, you will hear the words of Jesus, "Well done, good and faithful servant; you were faithful over a few things, I will make you ruler over many things. Enter into the joy of your Lord" (Matthew 25:21).

—Pastor Dave Love

Chapter 1:

Salvation

This chapter will discuss the following topics:
The Cross and Salvation
Atonement: The Threefold Work of Christ Crucified
Propitiation, Redemption, and Reconciliation in the Bible
Propitiation Is Godward
Anger Versus Wrath
Redemption Is Sinward
Reconciliation Is Manward
Resurrection and Its Significance
The New Birth
Additional Benefits of the Finished Work of Salvation
Baptism, Discipleship, and Serving

Choosing to be discipled means that you have received the gift of salvation and eternal life through your faith in Jesus Christ. Salvation speaks of deliverance, from sin and its power, while also being delivered to a life in Jesus Christ. In other words, just as a newborn baby is delivered and handed over to the parents, we are delivered over to our Savior and Lord. The Apostle Paul speaks of our salvation as a threefold deliverance: "Yes, we had the sentence of death in ourselves, that we should not trust in ourselves but in God who raises the dead, who delivered us from so great a death, and does deliver us; in whom we trust that He will still deliver us" (2 Corinthians 1:9–10). The context of these verses is Paul's physical deliverance in Asia, but they give us a picture of our past, present, and future spiritual deliverance from sin and into life in Christ.

1. **Briefly describe your salvation experience. Why did you decide to trust in Jesus? List some of the changes God has made in your life so far.**

____

____

____

2. **Read about the salvation experience of the Philippian jailor and his family in Acts 16:25–34. What was required for his salvation (hint: verse 31)?**

____

____

____

3. **Read Romans 10:9–10. What are the components of salvation?**

____

____

____

When you first believe in your heart and then confess your faith in Christ to God, you are saved. It is important to understand the great sacrifice that was required for your salvation.

The Cross and Salvation

In Genesis 3:21 we see the first sacrifice of innocent animals to make coverings for Adam and Eve. This is due to their sin, which would ultimately result in their death. While the animal skins covered their bodies, the shed blood covered their sin. All sin is an offense to God and requires death, either of the sinner or a substitute, and because God is perfect and holy, He must deal with sin in relationship with mankind. In His great mercy and love, God put into place a sacrifice system that would atone (make amends) for sins committed and allow for people to still be in His presence and therefore in relationship with Him. Lambs, bulls, and goats were the typical sacrifices required in the Old Testament for sins.

However, it was a temporary system that required repeated sacrifices throughout a person's life because the substitutionary sacrifices never took away sin; they only covered it. The lamb was a type of foreshadowing of Jesus, for when Jesus came, John the Baptist pointed to Him, saying, "Behold! The Lamb of God who takes away the sin of the world!" (John 1:29). Jesus came down from heaven to Earth to be the one-time final sacrifice, whose death on the cross would pay for every person's sin for eternity. In Jesus, sins were not just covered, but they were taken away. Never again is another sacrifice required to appease God for those who receive Jesus.

Atonement: The Threefold Work of Christ Crucified

What specifically did Christ accomplish on the cross? His crucifixion forever changed our relationships with God, sin, and other people. His threefold work of propitiation, redemption, and reconciliation is like a three-legged stool. Each aspect of His work is connected to the cross, just like each leg of a stool is connected to the atonement seat. When we read in the Gospels about the six hours that Jesus hung on the cross, we do not see the words *propitiation*, *redemption*, or *reconciliation*. However, in the rest of the New Testament, we do see these three words, giving us a better understanding of what happened on the cross.

4. **Do you think any of your sins or someone else's sins are unforgivable? If yes, explain why?**

____

____

____

5. **Read 1 Peter 1:18–21. This passage shows the cost and benefits of our salvation. For whom did Jesus come? What is Peter teaching about the blood sacrifice of Christ?**

____

____

____

Atonement, the threefold work of Christ on the cross, is directional. First, it is Godward, directed toward God through _propitiation_, which is the appeasement of God's holiness or sinlessness. Next, it is Sinward, directed toward the sin of mankind. This is called _redemption_ since it is redeeming us from the bondage of sin. Lastly, it is Manward, directed toward the relationships between God and mankind. We first reconcile with God, which then provides the grounds for _reconciliation_ with each other.

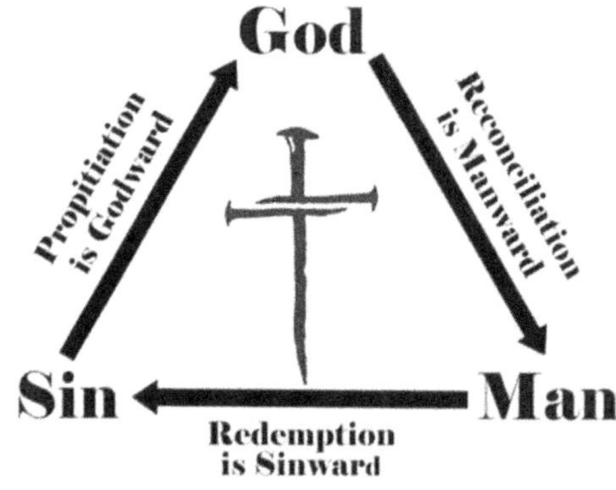

Propitiation, Redemption, and Reconciliation in the Bible

Propitiation (Godward)

God is free to forgive because His holiness has been appeased.	Rom. 3:25; Heb. 2:17
Humanity is delivered from the kingdom of darkness, removed from enemy status.	Col. 1:13; Eph. 2:1–3
Humanity is translated (or conveyed) into the Kingdom of God. Though sojourners on earth, we are placed into His Kingdom.	Col. 1:13
We are a royal Priesthood, not only a priesthood representing the people before God.	1 Pet. 2:5, 9; Rev. 1:6
We are a Special People because we are a chosen generation, a royal priesthood, a holy nation; we are different from the world.	1 Pet. 2:9; Titus 2:14
As heavenly Citizens, though sojourners on earth, our citizenship and our Kingdom is Heaven.	Phil. 3:20
We are lights in the world since we go from enemies and darkness to light bearers in the world.	Eph. 5:8; Phil. 2:15
We are made alive, emphasizing that we were dead but are now alive through faith because God is satisfied by the cross.	Col. 2:13; Eph. 2:1
We are brought near to God solely by the finished work of Christ. We who were afar off are brought near unto God.	Eph. 2:13

Redemption (Sinward)

We are redeemed from all aspects of sin's penalty and bondage.	Heb. 9:28; 2 Cor.1:10
We are forgiven from all trespasses and sins.	Eph. 1:7; Col. 2:13
The Christian is free as a believer to walk in the newness of life. The cross enables God to deal with the sin nature of the believer because it has been judged, though not eliminated.	Rom. 6:1–10; Phil. 2:12–13
We are justified and righteous, not just forgiven but made righteous and declared justified before God.	Rom. 5:1–9; 2 Cor. 5:21; Rom. 3:21–26
We are Circumcised in Christ, because positionally "in Christ" the flesh has been put off.	Eph. 2:11–13; Col. 2:11; 3:8–11

Reconciliation (Manward)

As believers, **we are reconciled to God**.	2 Cor. 5:18–21; Col. 1:20–22
We are free from the law of Moses, for we are under grace.	Rom. 6:14; Gal. 5:18
As children of God, **we are reborn of God** with every right and title belonging to that position—an heir of God and a joint heir with Jesus Christ.	John 1:12–13; 1 John 3:2
We are adopted by God, and He views all believers as legal adults, heirs with Christ His Son, with a new body waiting at death or the rapture.	Eph. 1:4–5; Rom. 8:23
We are each accepted as a person before God because we are in Christ.	Acts 10:35; Eph. 1:6
We can draw near to God at anytime, anywhere, for access to grace.	Rom. 5:3; Heb. 4:16
We are secure on the Rock. Jesus is the Rock, and we are the house that is built on the Rock that can withstand all storms.	Matt. 7:24–27; 1 Cor. 3:9–15
As God's family members, we are not just citizens and a royal priesthood but members of the family and household of God.	Eph. 2:19; Gal. 6:10
We are a gift to the Godhead. We are the Father's and we are the Son's.	John 17:6–12
We are vitally united to each other and to the Father, Son, and Holy Spirit as the Godhead is united to each other.	John 14:20; Rom. 12:5
We have a future guarantee, for we have received the Spirit as a guarantee or down payment for future graces, including a new body, our inheritance, and glorification.	2 Cor. 1:22; Eph. 1:13–14; 2 Cor. 5:5
We possess every spiritual blessing, as spiritual blessings are not material; they are the spiritual graces of God, our Father, to us.	Eph. 1:3

In the New Testament letters, we find these three words repeated: Propitiation, Redemption, and Reconciliation. Once we understand these words, we can begin to comprehend what happened during the six hours on the cross.

Propitiation Is Godward

Simply put, all sin is first against God. The sacrifice of Christ propitiates (satisfies) and appeases our God, against whom we have all sinned (Psalm 41:4; 51:4).

The word *propitiation* in our Bibles is from the Greek word *hilasterion*, which means mercy seat, propitiation, or appeasement. Propitiation as a part of Christ's sacrifice focuses on the holiness, the sinlessness of God. Since God is holy, He cannot and will not tolerate sin. He demands that we be holy, for He is holy or sinless (Leviticus 11:44; 1 Peter 1:16). Sin must be punished because sin is against God Himself. Through Jesus' shed blood on the cross, all our sins, past, present, and future, are taken away (Hebrews 9:26–28; 1 John 3:5). Through the lens of His blood, believers are viewed as holy by God. Therefore, God's requirement for holiness has been satisfied, and His wrath has been withheld until the Great Tribulation.

In the Old Testament the word *propitiation* is not found, but the concept is seen in the Mercy Seat, which covers the Ark of the Covenant (Leviticus 16:2). The Ark was a box kept in the Holy of Holies, which contained the Ten Commandments. These holy laws reflect God's holy nature and His will for mankind. Since the Jews were unable to keep God's laws perfectly, it was necessary that the blood of an animal sacrifice be sprinkled on the Mercy Seat once a year to cover their sins. The blood temporarily satisfied, or appeased, God's requirement for holiness, but the long-term solution to pay for our sins could not be met with the blood of animals. Only a perfect human being could propitiate, or satisfy, God's requirement for human holiness. God sent His Son, the perfect God-man, to be the propitiation for our sins. He came as the Lamb of God (Leviticus 16:14–15; Hebrews 9:11–14) and shed His blood on the cross so that all our sins, past, present, and future, were no longer temporarily covered but permanently taken away for those who believe (Hebrews 10:11; 1 John 3:5). From that time onward, God began to see all believers as holy, even those who by faith put their hope in the Messiah to come. Therefore, God's requirement for holiness was satisfied, or propitiated, through the blood sacrifice of Christ on the cross.

Read Luke 18:10–14.

In Luke 18:13, the Greek text literally reads, "God, be merciful [or make propitiation] to me a sinner!" or "God, be my mercy seat." In other words, "God, cover my sins because I am a sinner." Here we discover that the tax collector recognized that his sin was first against God, and it is only God who could cover his sin.

6. **In the New Testament the English word propitiation is used four times. Read and record what you learn about propitiation.**

Romans 3:21–25 ____

____

Hebrews 2:17 ____

____

1 John 2:2 ____

____

1 John 4:10 ____

____

Though church history often teaches that propitiation satisfies an angry God, we know that this is not the case. An angry God would never say He loves us and then prove His love by sending His only Son to die for us. God's holiness (sinlessness) is appeased or satisfied with the sacrifice of Jesus Christ. This is propitiation.

Propitiation
Our sins against God are satisfied by the sacrifice of Jesus Christ.

Click for further study on propitiation.

Anger Versus Wrath

What is the difference between God's anger and God's wrath? Anger is a strong expression of displeasure toward someone. The words *angry* and *anger* are used to refer to God only three times in the New Testament (Hebrews 3:10, 17 and Mark 3:5). In all uses, unbelief and hardness of

Jewish hearts were cited for why He was angry. After the propitiation of the cross, we do not read of God being angry with believers in the Church Age in which we live. Instead, Romans 5:9 speaks of our being saved from God's wrath. Wrath expresses the righteous judgment of God upon those who reject His Son in unbelief. God's abiding wrath toward unrepentant sinners is spoken of many times throughout the New Testament, but He is rich in mercy, very long-suffering, and forbearing. God is holding back His wrath in this Age of Grace (Romans 2:4; Ephesians 2:3–4) until the seven-year Tribulation and Judgment when He will pour out His wrath on unbelievers.

7. **Read John 3:36. What happens if you don't believe in Jesus?**

____

____

Redemption Is Sinward

Redemption deals with sin itself, which is the root cause of what offended God's holiness and has held mankind in bondage. Ever since Adam's choice to disobey God in the Garden of Eden, sin has become the master of mankind, along with sin's originator, Satan. Because we have a sin nature, we often choose our ways over God's ways, and the penalty for these choices is bondage here and eternal death to come. God, in His great love for mankind, provided redemption from sin by sending His Son, Jesus Christ, to sacrifice Himself on the cross. The shedding of His blood paid the penalty for our sin and freed us from the power and bondage of sin and Satan, who desires to enslave us (Ephesians 2:1–3). Believers in Jesus are no longer destined to eternal death due to sin because Jesus redeemed us when He paid the price for our sin by dying on the cross.

Scan this QR Code for further study on Redemption.

The basic New Testament Greek words for *redeem* and *redemption* are *agorazo* and *lutrao*. *Agorazo* and its derivatives basically mean to ransom in the marketplace of humanity. *Lutrao* emphasizes setting free what has been ransomed or purchased, from the power and bondage of sin and Satan. Once a person is purchased, he or she is freed from bondage while remaining in the world as a citizen of heaven. The final act of redemption will be the redemption of our bodies in heaven (Romans 8:23; 1 Corinthians 15:42–44).

8. **Read Romans 6:6–23, Colossians 1:14, and Hebrews 2:14–15. What conclusions can you draw about Jesus paying the penalty for your sin?**

____

____

9. **Read John 3:16–18 and explain how this payment becomes effective in your life.**

____

____

Reconciliation Is Manward

Man's relationship with God is made possible by Jesus' death on the cross. The relationship between man and God in the garden of Eden was broken due to sin. To restore this relationship, a change needed to occur. However, in the stubbornness of his sin, mankind did not want to change his ways and did not seek reconciliation with God. It was God, in His great mercy and love, who reached out to us to restore our relationship with Him through Jesus.

The New Testament Greek words for *reconciliation* are the noun *katallage* (Romans 5:11; 11:15; 2 Corinthians 5:18–19) and the verb *katallasso* (Romans 5:10; 1 Corinthians 7:11; 2 Corinthians 5:18–20). Reconciliation means a change of relationship from hostility to harmony and peace between two parties. Reconciliation is first with God and then between two or more people. Because God does not change nor does He need to change, the change must occur with us. Since we could not and would not change on our own, God did the unimaginable and provided a way to restore mankind's relationship with Him—if we would believe in what Jesus did on the cross. Now reconciliation with God is available to everyone.

10. **Read 2 Corinthians 5:18–21. Notice that reconciliation is from God to us and from us to others. What is the message of reconciliation we should share with others?**

____

____

Through Christ's death on the cross, God is propitiated, sinners are redeemed, and mankind is reconciled to God.

Scan this QR Code for further study on Reconciliation.

We know God the Father accepted Jesus' sacrifice because God resurrected the Son from the dead!

Resurrection and Its Significance

Christ's sacrificial death on the cross was critical for our salvation, and His resurrection from the dead was also critical. None of the animal sacrifices offered under the Law of Moses were ever raised from the dead because they could not take away sins but only temporarily cover them (Hebrews 10:4, 11).

11. **Read Acts 2:22–24 and Romans 6:23. Why could death not hold Christ?**

____

____

12. Read Romans 4:23–25. Why was He raised from the dead?

____

____

13. Read 1 Corinthians 15:12–17. If Christ did not rise from the dead, what pre-dicament would we be in?

____

____

____

Jesus' resurrection certified that God accepted Christ's "once for all" sacrifice. Now God is just and holy in declaring those who believe in the risen Christ as righteous.

Bridge

The Father accepted the sacrifice of Jesus by raising Him from the dead. As a result, we are forgiven, made right before God, and born again.

The New Birth

Once we believe in the finished work of Christ crucified, God begins to change us. We begin to understand that God not only fixes our sin problems by forgiving us, redeeming us, and reconciling us, but He also loves to create new people. No longer are we tied to the likeness of the first Adam; now we are free to be remade into the likeness of the last Adam, Jesus Christ (1 Corinthians 15:45–49). As 2 Corinthians 5:17 says, "Therefore, if anyone is in Christ, he is a new creation; old things have passed away; behold, all things have become new." The new person still resides in the old body but now with the added 24/7 presence of the Holy Spirit, who is constantly working to change us into the image of Christ. At death we will put off our earthly body and put on a new body, fit for heaven (2 Corinthians 5:1–8).

14. **Jesus declared that we must be born a second time. Read John 3:1–16 and 1 Peter 1:23–25; then explain in your own words how the new birth comes about.**

____

____

____

Bridge

Now that we have a better understanding of the finished work of Christ, let's discover some of the benefits of His work in our new lives.

Additional Benefits of the Finished Work of Salvation

Grace

Grace is different from both mercy and love. Notice that all three words are used in Ephesians 2:4–5, each with its own separate meaning: "But God, who is rich in mercy [His forbearance and long-suffering], because of His great love [His motivation] with which He loved us, even when we were dead in trespasses, made us alive together with Christ (by grace [His undeserved favor] you have been saved)." We see from these verses how these three words work together and how they are different.

Some simple definitions of grace:

> Grace means undeserved kindness. It is the gift of God to man the moment he sees he is unworthy of God's favor.
>
> — Dwight L. Moody

> Grace is God giving us what we don't deserve.
>
> — Dan Roberts

> GRACE: God's Riches At Christ's Expense.
>
> — Old Sunday school definition

The finished work of Christ unleashes God's grace to save us, and it enables us to be and do all that we should be and do as newly born children of God. We have been saved through our faith. Ephesians 2:8 tells us, "For by grace you have been saved through faith, and that not of yourselves; it [salvation] is the gift of God." Faith comes to us through receiving the Word of God (Romans 10:17). Just like Timothy describes in 1 Timothy 4:6, we can be "nourished in the words of faith and of the good doctrine." Scripture teaches about the manifold gifts of grace that we receive from God when we are saved by grace through faith. The Greek word for manifold is *poikilos*, which means various or variety. We find this word *manifold* in 1 Peter 4:10, so "manifold grace" means the many gifts of grace that come from God through faith. When we receive Jesus by faith, we receive many gifts of grace that are common to all believers. For example, forgiveness, God's mercy, being filled with the Holy Spirit, peace with God, being a child of God, being sealed by the Holy Spirit, and many others.

Scan this QR Code for further study on Grace.

15. **Explain how God has shown you grace in your life.**

____

____

____

16. **Read Romans 12:6–8 and 1 Peter 4:10–11. Write down the gifts of grace in these verses and what our responsibility is with regards to them toward each other and God.**

____

____

____

____

Repentance

We live in a sinful body in a sinful world, and we need to repent often throughout our lives. Repentance is the Greek word *metanoia*, which means a change of mind that leads to a change of direction in your life, leading to a changed life. Do not mistake sorrow alone for repentance; in other words, a repentant heart and mind mean more than feeling bad about sin.

17. **Read 2 Corinthians 7:10–11, Jeremiah 25:5, and Ezekiel 18:30. What is required for repentance?**

____

____

____

____

Repentance, or a change of mind, is a step toward forgiveness and change. First John 1:9 reads, "If we confess our sins, He is faithful and just to forgive us our sins and to cleanse us from all unrighteousness." The word *repentance* is not found in this verse, and yet repentance has occurred. How so? Confession implies a change of mind that brought us to the place of admitting that what we have thought, said, or done is wrong. By confessing it to God, we are asking for forgiveness, which He faithfully grants.

18. **Read Luke 15:10–24. When did repentance occur in this parable? How do we know it was true repentance?**

____

____

____

____

Repentance is a change of mind followed by corresponding action.

— C. I. Scofield

Love, Forgiveness, and Justification

When we repent and turn to God, we come face-to-face with His love, forgiveness, and justification. God is love; therefore, He is the source and starting point of all love. His great love for us led Him to forgive our sins through faith in His Son Jesus and to justify us. God now looks at us as if we never sinned.

19. **Read 1 John 4:8. What do you learn about God in this verse?**

____

____

____

20. **Read Romans 4:1–8. How was Abraham justified? How are we justified?**

____

____

____

Forgiveness and justification are two sides of one coin called redemption. Forgiveness is taking away sin, and justification is being declared righteous by God. Both happen immediately when we believe in the finished work of Christ. Justification is a declaration that Christ's righteousness is now the believer's righteousness, and the believer is no longer in danger of being cast into the Lake of Fire. Jesus Christ's righteousness is like a royal garment put on us by God; it is ours now forever and can never be taken away.

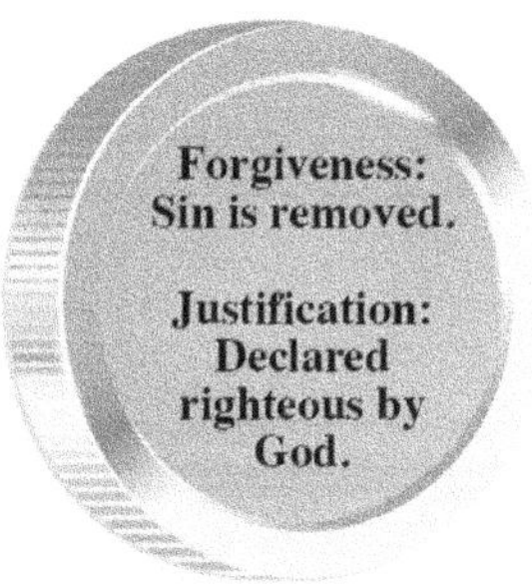

Forgiven and justified disciples love God and others. The more we understand how much we have been forgiven, the more we will love.

We need to receive God's love and forgiveness for ourselves first, then demonstrate our love for God by extending forgiveness and love to our brothers and sisters in Christ and to our enemies.

21. **Read 1 John 3:16. How do we demonstrate love for others and what does that look like?**

____

____

____

22. **Read Luke 6:27 and Romans 12:17–21. How should we respond to our enemies?**

____

____

____

23. **Read Luke 7:36–50. The word forgiven used by Jesus in verse 48 is in the perfect tense, meaning the woman was forgiven of her sins some time prior to her finding Him at the Pharisees house. When she realized that her forgiveness was complete, she sought Jesus out to thank and worship Him. Explain why the woman was worshipping and loving Jesus while the Pharisee was not.**

____

____

____

24. **Read Ephesians 4:32. Do you freely offer forgiveness to those who have offended you? Is there anyone you have not been able to forgive? If yes, why? Reflect on Jesus' sacrifice and remember that Jesus forgave you.**

____

____

____

25. **Read 1 John 4:20–21. What is the connection between loving God and loving others? From these verses, how serious is God about loving each other when we say we love Him?**

____

____

____

____

Eternal Security and Assurance

Eternal Security and Assurance of Salvation are related but different. Eternal Security is a factual matter. It means that once saved, a believer in Christ crucified cannot lose his or her salvation, either by committing a specific sin or sins or by ceasing to believe. Even for those who think that they can lose their salvation, the fact is, they cannot lose it. The work of regeneration in a person's heart cannot be undone. It is the work of the Holy Spirit and God that keeps the believer safe and secure and not the efforts of the saved person.

The doctrine of Eternal Security depends on what God has done on our behalf. If a person can lose his or her salvation, then certain works of God would have to be undone or reversed.

26. **Read 1 Corinthians 12:13. What would have to be reversed to lose your salvation?**

____

27. **Read Ephesians 1:13, 4:30. What would have to be broken to lose our salvation?**

____

28. **How long does the seal last?**

____

The possibility of being unbaptized or unsealed is not taught in the Scriptures. It is the Father's purpose to keep us secure regardless of any efforts to remove us from His hands (John 10:28–30; 13:1). Ultimately, He will present us faultless in His own presence (Jude 24), where our physical state will match our perfect standing in Christ.

29. **Read Hebrews 7:25. *Uttermost* means completely or forever. How long is your salvation?**

30. **Read Romans 8:29–39. List the ways that God makes your salvation eternally secure.**

Assurance of Salvation is the confident belief that you are truly saved. It means that no matter how you feel and regardless of your personal struggles with sin, you rely on the fact that you are a child of God through faith in Jesus Christ, destined to eternal life in glory. There are several reasons we can be confident in our salvation, and the first is the Word of God. The Bible teaches that we can be sure that we are saved, and it is our responsibility to believe it.

31. **Read 1 John 5:13. What does this tell us about our assurance of salvation?**

32. **Read Hebrews 10:19–23. What do these verses teach us about the assurance of our salvation?**

These and other scriptures are the foundation of our assurance (Isaiah 32:17, Hebrews 6:11; 10:22; 1 Thessalonians 1:5; Colossians 2:2).

The second reason we can have assurance is the work of the Holy Spirit in our lives. "The Spirit himself bears witness with our spirit, that we are the children of God" (Romans 8:16). Assurance is therefore not presumption; it is a tested and confident faith.

The third reason is the evidence of works in our own lives. When we are truly saved, it will be seen in the way we live. While works do not save us, the saved will produce works. These works contribute to an assurance of our salvation (James 2:14–18; 1 John 2:3–5; 1 John 3:14).

Relationship Versus Fellowship

Christians believe Jesus shed His blood on the cross for our sins. This places us immediately and forever into a personal relationship with God (John 1:12–13). That relationship is based on blood, and no one can take that away. However, just like with family, there are good and bad relationships. You might have a family member you haven't talked to in years, but you are still related. No one can ever take that away.

Fellowship is different. Fellowship with God and others speaks of joint participation, intimacy, oneness, closeness, and having things in common. As believers, fellowship is about following the Lord, day by day, as He directs your steps. If you do not follow where He leads and do not obey Him, then you do not experience intimate fellowship with God. Thankfully, broken fellowship can be quickly restored when we confess our sins and purpose to follow Him (1 John 1:6–9).

Living in relationship with God and walking in fellowship with Him each day brings fullness of joy and is God's will for all believers.

If you feel far from God, guess who moved?

Bridge

Now that we understand redemption, reconciliation, and propitiation, we will see what follows personal salvation.

Baptism, Discipleship, and Serving

Baptism

33. **Read Matthew 28:19–20. What are the two steps in making disciples?**

____

____

____

34. **Read Romans 6:4. What does baptism represent?**

____

____

Baptism was a common Jewish practice long before it became a Christian practice. The basic Hebrew meaning of *baptism* is identification. When baptized, you identify with a person, message, and/or group. When a Gentile converted to Judaism, he would be baptized to identify himself with Judaism and the Jewish people.

Baptism is an act of obedience to God. As we go under the water and come up again, it is a picture of identifying with Christ's death, burial, and resurrection, and of dying to the power of our old life and rising again to new life in Christ. Baptism is the outward declaration to the family of God of the inward transformation of faith in Jesus. Baptism does not save you because it is a work; however, it is necessary for obedience.

Discipleship

Discipleship is a lifelong process, and we are called to study and apply the Word of God. However, it's not enough to just study and grow in knowledge; obedience is what makes us a true disciple of Jesus. Furthermore, not only are we called to be a disciples, but we should also make disciples of others.

Obedience makes us a true disciple of Jesus

All the things that Jesus commanded us to observe, we learn about in the Gospels and in the Letters to the Churches. All the teachings that the Apostles received directly from Jesus and from His Spirit, after He ascended to Heaven, are now known as The Apostles' Doctrine.

35. **Read Acts 2:42. What do you learn about making disciples?**

____

____

____

Serving

Jesus did not come to be served but to serve. We, too, are to serve others at church, at home, in our neighborhoods, and everywhere we go. Although serving doesn't come naturally, Philippians 2:3–4 tells us that it requires humility to look out for the interests of others.

36. **Read Matthew 20:26–28 or Mark 10:44–45. What does Jesus teach us about serving?**

____

____

____

37. **Read Luke 9:23. Picking up the cross refers to serving Christ even when it is difficult. How does denying yourself relate to serving?**

____

____

____

38. **Read Luke 10:38–42. What is the warning here regarding serving?**

____

____

Those who serve continue to be discipled, but our flesh, our old nature, resists serving anyone but ourselves. That is why we require everyone who serves at Calvary Castle Rock to also attend a regular service.

Summary and Transition to Chapter 2

Our salvation is by grace through faith and is only possible because of the finished work of Christ crucified. The atonement that has come because of His cross is first directed Godward in propitiation. His sacrifice redeems us sinward, taking on sin's penalty, power, and presence. With God's holiness appeased and sin judged, God and Mankind can now be reconciled, and a relationship with God is now possible through faith.

We understand that Jesus' resurrection certifies His sacrifice and has been accepted by God the Father. His resurrection also provides new life, new creation within, and creates new children of God. We are now baptized out of obedience, to identify as disciples, and to be servants of Jesus. Chapter 2 will look at the key person who made our salvation possible. His name and title is Jesus Christ.

Chapter 2:

The Person of Jesus Christ

This chapter will discuss the following topics:
YHWH Is God
Jesus Is YHWH
Jesus Is God
Jesus Is the Messiah, Son of God
Jesus Is Human
Jesus Is the Most Unique Person Ever

We started this discipleship book with an overview of our salvation, looking at the sacrifice required to make our eternal salvation possible. Now we need to look at the person who sacrificed Himself, Jesus Christ, to understand who He is, His deity (God), and His humanity. If we take away either of those natures, then He is not Jesus, the Christ, of the Bible.

To establish the Deity of Jesus Christ we must also establish the fact that He is YHWH. YHWH is the personal name of God in the Old Testament (Isaiah 42:8; Jeremiah 16:21). We must first answer the question "Is YHWH God?" Once we establish the deity of YHWH, we then can understand that Jesus is YHWH.

YHWH Is God

YHWH from the Hebrew text of the Old Testament is typically translated in our English Bibles as Lord or God with every letter capitalized. Do the Scriptures ever specifically declare that YHWH (Lord) is God? Yes. Deuteronomy 4:35–36 reads, "To you [Israel] it was shown that you might know that the Lord [YHWH] Himself is God; there is none other besides Him. Out of heaven He let you hear His voice, that He might instruct you; on earth He showed you His great fire, and you heard His words out of the midst of the fire."

Verse 39 continues, "Therefore know this day, and consider it in your heart, that the Lord Himself is God in heaven above and on the earth beneath; there is no other" (see also Joshua 22:34 and 1 Kings 18:39).

1. **Read 1 Kings 8:60–61 and Psalms 100:3. Is YHWH only the God of Israel?**

____

____

YHWH is God, and whoever the Scriptures identify as YHWH is God.

Bridge

The truths of the Bible were revealed progressively by the Spirit over hundreds of years. This means that as we move from Genesis to Revelation, certain concepts and ideas become more and more fully developed. In the Old Testament we learned that the Messiah is YHWH, translated Lord or God. It wasn't until the New Testament that we know Him as Jesus. Even though Jesus was always one of the YHWH persons (i.e., Lord) in the Old Testament, most rabbis did not recognize the Messiah by this name.

Jesus Is YHWH

The Old Testament Scriptures make it abundantly clear that Jesus is YHWH, as the chart below shows.

Description of God	Verses	Description of Jesus	Verses
YHWH/I AM	Ex. 3:14–15; Isa. 43:10	I AM	John 8:24, 58; 18:4–6
God	Deut. 6:4; Josh. 8:30; Isa. 40:28	God	John 1:1,14; 20:28; Titus 2:13; Heb. 1:8; 2 Pet. 1:1
First and Last	Isa. 41:4; 48:12	First and Last Alpha and Omega	Rev. 1:8; 1:17–18; 2:8; 22:12–16
Lord	Ex. 4:10; Deut. 9:26; Jud. 6:22; Ps. 35:22	Lord	Matt. 12:8; Acts 7:59–60; 10:36; Rom. 10:12; 1 Cor. 2:8; 12:3; Phil. 2:10–11
Savior	Ps. 106:21; Isa. 43:3; 63:8; Luke 1:47; 1 Tim. 4:10; Jude 1:25	Savior	Luke 2:11; John 4:42; Titus 2:13; 3:6
King	Ps. 95:3; Isa. 43:15; 1 Tim. 6:14–16	King	John 18:37; Rev. 17:14; 19:16
Judge	Gen. 18:25; Ps. 50:4, 6; 96:13	Judge	John 5:22; Rom. 14:10; 2 Cor. 5:10; 2 Tim. 4:1
Light	2 Sam. 22:29; Ps. 27:1	Light	Isa. 42:6; John 1:4; 1:9; 3:19; 8:12; 9:5
Rock	Deut. 32:3–4; 2 Sam. 22:32; Ps. 89:26	Rock	Rom. 9:33; 1 Cor. 10:1–4; 1 Pet. 2:4–8
Redeemer	Ps. 78:35; Isa. 48:17; 54:5; 63:16	Redeemer	Rom. 3:24; Gal. 3:13; Eph. 1:7; Heb. 9:12
Our Righteousness	Isa. 45:24	Our Righteousness	Jer. 23:6; Rom. 3:21–22
Husband	Isa. 54:5; Hos. 2:16	Husband (Betrothed)	Matt. 25:1; Mark 2:18–19; 2 Cor. 11:2; Eph. 5:25–32; Rev 21:2, 9
Shepherd	Ps. 23:1; 80:1; 95:7	Shepherd	John 10:11, 16; Heb. 13:20; 1 Pet. 2:25; 5:4
Creator	Gen 1:1; Ps. 95:5–6; 102:25; Isa. 40:28; 42:5	Creator	John 1:2–3, 10; Col. 1:15–16; Heb. 1:10
Giver of Life	Gen 2:7; Deut. 32:39; 1 Sam. 2:6; Ps. 36:9	Giver of Life	John 5:21; 10:28; 11:25
Forgiver of Sin	Ex. 34:6–7; Neh. 9:17; Dan. 9:9	Forgiver of Sin	Mark 2:1–12; Acts 26:15–18; Col. 2:13; 3:13

Description of God	Verses	Description of Jesus	Verses
Lord Our Healer	Ex. 15:26	Healer	Acts 9:34
Omnipresent	Ps. 139:7–12; Prov. 15:3	Omnipresent	Matt. 18:20; 28:19–20; Acts 17:26–27; Eph. 4:10
Omniscient	1 Kings 8:39; Ps. 147:5; Jer. 17:9–10; 1 John 3:20	Omniscient	John 2:24–25; 21:15–19; Acts 1:24; Rom.11:33–36
Omnipotent	Isa. 40:10–31; Neh. 9:6	Omnipotent	Matt. 28:18; John 10:17–18; Col. 1:17; Heb. 1:3; 1 Pet. 3:22
Preexistent	Gen. 1:1	Preexistent	John 1:1, 14; 3:13; 6:62; 17:5
Eternal	Ps. 102:26–27; Hab. 3:6	Eternal	Isa. 9:6; Mic. 5:2; John 8:58
Immutable	Num. 23:19; Mal. 3:6; James 1:17	Immutable	Heb. 6:18; 7:24; 13:8
Receiver of Worship	Ps. 97:6–7; 99:5; Matt. 4:10; John 4:24; Rev. 7:11; 11:16	Receiver of Worship	Matt. 14:33; 28:9; John 9:38; Phil. 2:9–11; Heb. 1:6; Rev. 5:14
Speaker with Divine Authority	Ex. 8:1; Isa. 28:16; Hag. 1:7	Speaker with Divine Authority	Matt. 5:18; 7:28-29, John 3:3; 6:47; 8:58

Jesus Is God

Many ask the question "Does God exist?" but the question of whether Jesus Christ existed is asked by relatively few people. Most accept that Jesus was a real man who lived in Israel over two thousand years ago. The debate begins with a discussion of Jesus' full identity. While almost every major religion teaches that Jesus was a prophet, a good teacher, or a godly man, The Bible tells us that Jesus is infinitely more; He is the Son of God!

2. **Read Matthew 16:13–14. Who did the people say Jesus was?**

____

____

____

3. **Read Matthew 16:15–17. Who did the disciples say Jesus was?**

I am trying here to prevent anyone from saying the really foolish thing that people often say about Him [Jesus Christ]: "I'm ready to accept Jesus as a great moral teacher, but I don't accept his claim to be God." That is the one thing we must not say. A man who was merely a man and said the sort of things that Jesus said would not be a great and moral teacher. He would either be a lunatic - on a level with a man who says he is a poached egg - or else he would be the Devil of hell. You must make your choice. Either this man was, and is, the Son of God, or else a madman or something worse. You can shut him up for a fool, you can spit at him and kill him as a demon; or you can fall at his feet and call him Lord and God. But let us not come up with any patronizing nonsense about his being a great human teacher. He has not left that option open to us. He did not intend to.

— *C. S. Lewis (Mere Christianity)*

How do we know that Jesus is God?

Since God is YHWH and Jesus is YHWH, therefore Jesus is God according to:

Deuteronomy 6:4. "Hear, O Israel: The LORD our God, the LORD is one!"

(YHWH) (Elohim) (YHWH)

(singular) (plural)(singular)

If God is YHWH and YHWH is One, then Jesus is God because Jesus is also LORD and YHWH.

Description of God	Verses	Description of Jesus	Verses
God/YHWH/I AM	Ex. 3:14–15; Isa. 43:10	I AM	John 8:24; 8:58, 18:4–6
Savior	Ps. 106:21; Isa. 43:3; 63:8; Luke 1:47; 1 Tim. 4:10; Jude 1:25	Savior	Luke 2:11; John 4:42; Titus 2:13; 3:6
King	Ps. 95:3; Isa. 43:15; 1 Tim. 6:14–16	King	John 18:37; Rev. 17:14; 19:16
Redeemer	Ps. 78:35; Isa. 48:17; 54:5; 63:16	Redeemer	Rom. 3:24; Gal. 3:13; Eph. 1:7; Heb. 9:12
Creator	Gen 1:1; Ps. 95:5–6; 102:25; Isa. 40:28; 42:5	Creator	John 1:2–3, 10; Col. 1:15–16; Heb. 1:10

Jesus Is God Because He Claimed to Be

When God called Moses to lead His people out of Egypt, Moses asked, "Who shall I say sent me?"

4. **Read Exodus 3:13–14. Who does God say that He is?**

____

____

5. **Read John 8:21–30. In verse 28 "He" is italicized, meaning it is not in the Greek text; this should read "I AM." Knowing this, who does Christ say that He is?**

____

____

Prebirth existence is an attribute only of God, and Jesus claimed it. He also identified Himself as God manifested in the flesh by claiming He is the "I AM."

6. **Read John 8:56–59. How did the Jews react to this astonishing statement from Jesus?**

____

____

7. Read John 10:30–33. Why did the Jews want to stone Jesus?

New Testament Writers Referred to Jesus as God

8. Read John 1:1–4 and 1:14. How did John describe Jesus?

9. Read John 20:28. How did Thomas address Jesus? Notice that Jesus did not correct him.

Granville Sharp Rule: A Greek grammatical construction in which two nouns are connected by καί (and the conjunction and), but only the first noun is preceded by the definite article "the". If the noun is impersonal, plural, or proper name, they share a unity, equality or even identity of reference.

Example:

I met "the" owner and "the" Chef of the new restaurant.
(2 separate people)

I met "the" owner and chef of the new restaurant. (The same person)

10. Read Titus 2:13. How did Paul describe Jesus?

11. Read 2 Peter 1:1. What did Peter call Jesus?

The Father Declared Jesus to be God

12. **Read Psalm 45:6 and Hebrews 1:8. What does the Father say about the deity of Jesus?**

____

____

____

13. **Read Romans 1:3. What does this verse state about Jesus?**

____

____

____

14. **Read Hebrews 12:2. Where is Jesus today?**

____

____

____

15. **Read Matthew 22:41–46. What is Jesus teaching here about Himself?**

____

____

____

16. **Read Acts 2:29–36. What is Peter telling the Jews about Jesus?**

____

____

____

Why is the question of Jesus' divine identity so important? Why does it matter that Jesus is the Son of God? Below are several reasons.

If Jesus is not God, then Jesus is a liar and is untrustworthy in every way. No sane person, who is not God, would say the things that He said. Jesus is either who He said He is, the Son of God manifest in the flesh, or He is a liar and a lunatic.

17. **Read John 6:29–40. What is Jesus saying about where He comes from (vv. 29 and 33)?**

____

____

18. **Who does Jesus claim to be working for (vv. 38 and 40)?**

____

____

____

19. **What is His mission on Earth (v. 40)?**

____

____

____

20. **Read John 14:6. What is Jesus declaring here?**

____

____

____

If Jesus is not God, then the apostles were also liars, and they would have been martyred for a lunatic man who was and is dead! According to church history, all the Apostles except John were martyred for their belief that Jesus was God and that He rose from the dead.

If Jesus is not God, His death would not have been sufficient to pay the penalty for the sins of the whole world. First John 2:2 says, "And He Himself is the propitiation for our sins, and not for ours only but also for the whole world."

21. **Read Genesis 22:8, John 3:16, Romans 5:8, and 2 Corinthians 5:21. What do these verses say about God's provision in His sacrifice?**

____

____

____

If Jesus is not God, then why do both God and Jesus say they are the Savior? God is the only Savior. Hosea 13:4 says, "Yet I am the LORD your God ever since the land of Egypt, and you shall know no God but Me; for there is no savior besides Me."

22. **Read 1 Timothy 2:3 and Titus 2:13. If Jesus is the Savior, what must we conclude about His divinity?**

____

____

____

YHWH is God

Jesus is YHWH

Therefore, Jesus is God

Bridge

The Son of God existed before He became a man, and we see Him appear throughout the Old Testament.

Old Testament Appearances of Christ

The phrase The Angel of the LORD" is found over fifty times in the Old Testament. These appearances are called Christophanies (appearances of Christ) or Theophanies (appearances of God). The Angel of the LORD is a manifestation of God that is tangible to human senses via the eyes, ears, and/or touch (1 John 1:1–2). He is a visible appearance of the Son of God, in human form, depicted in the Old Testament. The Angel of the LORD spoke as God, identified Himself as God, and exercised God's prerogatives.

23. **Read Exodus 3:1–6. In this notable example of a Christophany, how does God appear to Moses?**

---

24. **Who is in the burning bush, according to verses 2 and 6?**

Read Joshua 5:13–15.

In this passage God the Son appeared to Joshua before the battle of Jericho as Commander of the Lord's army. Notice that the phrase "The Angel of the Lord" is not used word for word here, but the verses clearly show that the Man was God. Why? Because Joshua fell down and worshiped Him, like in Moses' encounter where they were both standing on Holy Ground and only God was to be worshiped.

Discover other appearances of The Angel of the Lord" (i.e., Jesus) by reading the following verses: Genesis 12:7–9, Genesis 18:1–2, Genesis 32:22–30 with Hosea 12:4–5, and Deuteronomy 31:14–15.

25. **What are the different manifestations of the Angel of the Lord in these passages?**

A question often asked by believers is, "Are Christophanies or Theophanies always an appearance of the Second Person of the Trinity?" and the answer is yes.

26. **Read John 1:18, John 5:37, John 14:8–9, 1 Timothy 6:13–16, and Hebrews 1:1–3. Why do appearances of God in the Old Testament have to be considered to refer to the Son?**

____

____

____

Every Christophany or Theophany where God the Son takes on human form foreshadowed the incarnation. God the Son permanently took on human form to live among us as Emmanuel, meaning "God with us" (Matthew 1:23). There are no more Christophanies or Theophanies in the New Testament, and appearances of the Angel of the Lord ceased after the incarnation of Christ, so we can conclude that Jesus was the preincarnate Christ.

Why Wasn't the Father Ever Seen?

God the Father has revealed that no human in a sinful body could look upon God the Father and live because He dwells in unapproachable light. This echoes what the Lord (YHWH) said to Moses when he wanted to see His face:

> And he [Moses] said, "Please, show me Your glory." Then He [God] said, "I will make all My goodness pass before you, and I will proclaim the name of the Lord before you [the meanings of God's names help to describe Him]. I will be gracious to whom I will be gracious, and I will have compassion on whom I will have compassion." But He said, "You cannot see My face; for no man shall see Me, and live." And the Lord said, "Here is a place by Me, and you shall stand on the rock. So it shall be, while My glory passes by, that I will put you in the cleft of the rock and will cover you with My hand while I pass by. Then I will take away My hand, and you shall see My back; but My face shall not be seen." (Exodus 33:18–23)

First Timothy 6:16 similarly refers to "[God,] who alone has immortality, dwelling in unapproachable light, whom no man has seen or can see, to whom be honor and everlasting power. Amen."

27. **Read 1 Timothy 1:17 and John 4:24. What terms are used to describe God?**

____

____

____

Bridge

Jesus is the Son of God and became the Messiah. Now we will investigate His divine names, divine attributes, title, and role as the Messiah.

Jesus Is the Messiah, the Son of God

Messiah and Christ mean the same thing: the Anointed One. Messiah is a Hebrew title from the Old Testament, while Christ is from the Greek New Testament. The Apostle John explained the word *Messiah* in John 1:41: "'We have found the Messiah' (which is translated, the Christ)." John's immediate audience needed to know that Messiah and Christ meant the same thing, because many of them were not familiar with Hebrew words. As a divine title, both words refer to the same person, Jesus. The Anointed One is anointed and equipped for a purpose or mission.

> Messiah (Hebrew)
>
> Christ (Greek)
>
> Both mean the same thing:
>
> The Anointed One

The Messiah in the Old Testament is often seen as the coming conqueror and ruler.

28. **Read 1 Samuel 2:10 and Psalm 2. What is the description of this conquering Messiah?**

____

____

____

After Jesus was raised from the dead, He spoke to His disciples about how He had to suffer and die.

29. **Read Luke 24:44–46. Where is it written that the Messiah had to suffer and die?**

____

____

____

30. **Read Psalm 22:1–18 and Isaiah 52:13–53:12. How did the Messiah suffer?**

____

____

____

Linking the Son of God to the Messiah

In Matthew 16 we learn that Jesus brought His disciples to Caesarea Philippi. Up to this point, Jesus had healed people, cast out demons, calmed the storm, and cleansed the lepers. He fulfilled all the Messianic Miracles that were expected of the Messiah, the Christ. Now Jesus asks the disciples, "Who am I?"

31. **Read Matthew 16:13–16. What was Peter's response?**

____

____

____

32. **Read Romans 1:3–4. List the characteristics of Jesus as the Christ.**

Divine Names of the Messiah

Jesus was given names that pointed to the fact that He is God. There are seven divine names used of Jesus in the pages of the New Testament.

Titles of Christ	Descriptions	Verses
God	Jesus is called God.	John 20:28; Acts 20:28; 2 Pet. 1:1; Titus 2:13
Son of God	This is a divine name.	Matt. 16:16
Lord	Lord is used in the sense of God.	John 1:23; Acts 2:21; Rom. 10:13
The Alpha and the Omega	He is the beginning and the end of all things.	Rev. 1:8
The First and the Last	He always was in existence and always will be in existence.	Rev. 1:17
The Image of God	The images of God reveal and describe His reality.	Col. 1:15; Heb. 1:3
The Word (Greek: Logos)	The Logos, i.e., the Word, is the complete declaration of God.	John 1:1–14

Old and New Testament Comparisons of Divine Names

Now we will show the Old and New Testament references that apply to Jesus.

God

The Word is called God. John 1:1 says, "In the beginning was the Word, and the Word was with God, and the Word was God." This tells us that the Word existed from eternity, and the Word was distinct from God and was at the same time God Himself.

33. **33. Read John 1:14–17. Who is the Word?**

---

34. **Read 2 Corinthians 5:19. What is God doing in Christ?**

35. **Read Hebrews 1:8. How does the Father address the Son?**

We will take a closer look at Jesus' distinct personhood as God when we study the Trinity.

Son of God

In the Old Testament, there are Messianic quotes that refer to the Son, but the idea of Jesus as deity wasn't fully explained until the New Testament, when the Jewish writers described Him as the Son of God. They interpreted the Old Testament references to the Son as being fulfilled in Jesus Christ. The name Son of God was a Messianic title that emphasized His deity and His eternal relationship to the Father as Son.

36. **Read Isaiah 7:14. Then read Matthew 1:18–23 and Luke 1:34–35. Explain how these verses interpret Isaiah 7:14.**

37. **Read Luke 22:70 (as well as Matthew 26:62–64 and Mark 14:60–62). What title did Jesus confirm as His own?**

Lord

Another name for Jesus that emphasizes His deity is Lord. In the Bible, the word *lord* may be used either of men or of God. When Jesus is referred to as Lord, it means God and is often a translation of Old Testament passages where God's personal name, YHWH (translated in English as Lord), is used. In the New Testament it is translated as Lord, applied to Jesus, and is never applied to any other man.

38. **Read Joel 2:32. Lord has all four letters capitalized, which means it is the personal name YHWH. How does the Holy Spirit use Romans 10:9–13 to interpret Joel 2:32?**

39. **Read John 20:28. How does Thomas describe Jesus?**

Here are other Old Testament scriptures where the Holy Spirit connects Lord to Jesus:

> For this is He who was spoken of by the prophet Isaiah saying: "The voice of the one crying in the wilderness: 'Prepare the way of the Lord; Make His paths straight.'" (Matthew 3:3 quotes Isaiah 40:3)

> That at the name of Jesus every knee should bow, of those in heaven, and of those on earth, and of those under the earth, and that every tongue should confess that Jesus Christ is Lord, to the glory of God the Father. (Philippians 2:10–11 quotes from Isaiah 45:22–23)

The Alpha and the Omega, the First and the Last

In Revelation 22:13, Jesus gives us His last I AM declaration of the Scriptures. This statement reflects three very similar descriptive titles of Himself. The verse reads, "I am the Alpha and the Omega, the Beginning and the End, the First and the Last." Alpha and Omega are the first and last letters of the Greek alphabet. The next two phrases explain what Jesus means by calling Himself the first and last letters of the Greek alphabet. He explains by saying He is "the beginning and the end," and then He uses a similar phrase that is used in the Old Testament of YHWH, "the First . . . and the Last" (Isaiah 44:6). His I AM declarations echo what Paul said of Him in Romans 9:5: "Of whom are the fathers and from whom, according to the flesh, Christ came, who is over all, the eternally blessed God. Amen."

40. **Read Exodus 3:13–14. Who is I AM?**

____

____

____

41. **What is the significance of the four I AM statements in Revelation 1:8, 1:11, 21:6, and 22:13?**

____

____

42. **Read Hebrews 1:10. What do you learn about Jesus?**

____

____

43. **Read Isaiah 44:6 and Revelation 1:17. What is the connection between these verses?**

____

____

____

The Image of God

This title also emphasizes the deity of the Messiah. Colossians 1:15 says, "He [Jesus] is the image of the invisible God, the firstborn over all creation." The word *image* means prototype—in other words, the image in its physical and revealed reality. It is the visible manifestation of the invisible God. Additionally, Hebrews 1:3 says, "Who [the Son] being the brightness of His glory and the express image of His person, and upholding all things by the word of His power, when He had by Himself purged our sins, sat down at the right hand of the Majesty on high."

In this verse, a different Greek word for image is used, which means "an exact image," not just a likeness, but the exact image. This is an image like an impression made in clay, the clay will have an exact imprint of anything that is pressed into it. When Jesus is called the "express image," it means He has the exact impression of the divine nature or essence, not just a physical image. Since the Father is fully God, the Son is also fully God, and everything that is true of the divine nature of the Father is also true of the Son.

44. **Read John 14:8–9 and Hebrews 1:3. What are Jesus and the author of Hebrews saying here?**

____

____

____

The Word

The phrase "The Word" comes from the Greek word *Logos*. The root has the concept of thought, conception, expression, or utterance. The Word is the complete declaration of God. Jesus, who is the Word and is closest to God, has declared who He is (John 1:18).

The titles of Jesus show Him to be God. He is not only God by title, but He is also God according to His attributes.

The Divine Attributes of Jesus Christ

Attribute	Description	Verses
Eternality	Jesus exists both in the past and in the future.	John 8:58; Col. 1:17; Heb. 1:11
Immutability	He is changeless.	Heb. 1:10–12; Heb. 13:8

Self-Existence	He always existed.	John 5:26; John 1:1–3
Life in and of Himself	He has life and deity within Himself; He was not given life.	John 1:4; John 14:6; Acts 3:15
Holiness	He is sinless.	Heb. 7:26
Sovereignty	He is in total control, even within mankind's free will.	Matt. 5:27–28; Matt. 28:18; John 17:2
Omnipotent	He is all-powerful.	John 10:18; Luke 8:25; 1 Cor. 15:25–28; Phil. 3:21
Omniscience	He is all-knowing.	1 Cor. 4:5; Col. 2:3; Rev. 2:23
Omnipresent	He is present everywhere.	John 14:23; Rev. 3:20

Jesus is the Christ, the Messiah, and God according to the many divine attributes that He displayed by word and deed.

Moving on from the divinity of the Son, we will look now at His humanity. Jesus became the perfect substitute for mankind to satisfy God the Father.

Jesus Is Human

The Son, Jesus Christ, was always God. However, to be the perfect sacrifice for mankind, He also had to become a sinless Man. The Old Testament sacrificial system allowed the sins of the people to be temporarily covered by the shed blood of an animal. The death of the innocent animal acted as a substitute for the death of the guilty sinner. But this system could only cover the sin of mankind temporarily; it could not take it away permanently. Since it was the man (Adam) who sinned, only an innocent and perfect man could sacrifice Himself to remove sin once and for all. Yet no such mortal would ever exist, so God offered His divine Son as the perfect sacrifice, the Lamb of God. Only the shed blood of Jesus could atone for our sins, pay our debt, and open a way back to God for mankind. This is summed up in Romans 6:23: "For the wages of sin is death, but the gift of God is eternal life in Christ Jesus our Lord."

> Only His shed blood could atone for our sins, pay our debt, and open a way back to God for mankind.

Humanity of the Messiah, the Son of God

45. **Read John 6:33 and 38. Where does Jesus come down from? What did He come to do?**

____

____

____

46. **Read Isaiah 9:6. What did Jesus become when He came down from heaven?**

____

____

____

Jesus had always been God, specifically the Son of God, but before being born into this world, Jesus had never been a man. There are some who believe that God would never become a man. They believe that God, who is spirit, regards all things physical as evil. This is a form of Gnosticism, meaning that some have special knowledge that others do not have. Gnostics believe that the Jesus of the Gospels had a phantom body and was not really human, as indicated in Matthew 14:26. However, Jesus was a real human being with human attributes and characteristics, as many scriptures reveal.

Humanity of the Messiah Explained

Title	Description	Verses
Son of Man	He is called the Son of Man to emphasize His humanity.	Mark 2:27–28; John 5:27; 6:62
Son of David	This emphasizes His royalty by teaching that Jesus is a King from the royal line of David, and He fulfills the Davidic Covenant.	2 Sam. 7:12–16; Isa. 9:6–7; Jer. 23:5–6; Luke 1:30–33
Man of Sorrows	This is an Old Testament designation for the suffering Messiah.	Isa. 53:3

Title	Description	Verses
Last Adam	The first man, Adam, became a living being. The Last Adam became a life-giving spirit.	1 Cor. 15:45
Jesus of Nazareth	Of all the places to be raised, He grew up in one of the most denigrated towns.	Matt. 2:23; John 1:45–46
Rabbi	He was a Jewish teacher.	John 1:38; 3:2; 6:25
High Priest	His current ministry in Heaven on our behalf is as High Priest.	Heb. 4:15–16; Heb. 5:1; 5–6; Ps. 110:4
My Servant	Jesus equates this role with that of God's Servant.	Isa. 42:1–4; 43:10; Matt. 12:15–21; Mark 10:45

Son of Man

Jesus, the Son of God, is fully God and fully man. Of all His human titles, the most prominent is the Son of Man. It was His favorite title for Himself.

47. **Read John 3:13 and John 5:27. What do these verses tell us about the Son of Man?**

____

____

____

48. **Read Matthew 20:18–19 and verse 28. What are some of the sufferings Jesus experienced as a human?**

____

____

____

49. **Read Mark 2:27–28, John 5:25–27, and John 6:52–54. What areas of authority does Jesus have as the Son of Man?**

____

____

____

50. **Read Daniel 7:13–14 and Matthew 16:27. What do you learn about the future of the Son of Man?**

Son of David

Jesus is called the Son of David to emphasize both His royalty as King and His connection to the Davidic Covenant.

51. **Read Jeremiah 23:5–6. Describe what Jesus will do as King.**

The Davidic Covenant promises that a King from David's descendants would sit on David's throne. Jesus is under the Davidic Covenant because He Himself is a direct descendant of David, and He will be the One to finally fulfill it in Jerusalem.

52. **Read Isaiah 9:6–7 and Luke 1:30–33. What more do you learn about Jesus' fulfillment of the Davidic Covenant?**

Man of Sorrows

An Old Testament designation for the suffering Messiah is Man of Sorrows. Isaiah prophesied of the Suffering Messiah.

53. **Read Isaiah 52:13–53:12. List His many sorrows shown in these verses.**

---

54. **Can Jesus relate to your sorrows? Explain.**

____

____

____

Last Adam

There are only two Adams in the Bible. The first Adam was the father of the human race, as seen in Genesis 1:28. The second and last Adam, Jesus, is the head of all those in humanity who put their faith in Him.

55. **Read Romans 5:12–21 and 1 Corinthians 15:45. List the differences between the First and Last Adam and what each brings us.**

First Adam

Last Adam

56. **Read 1 Corinthians 15:45. What does the title "Last Adam" imply?**

____

____

____

Jesus of Nazareth

This title is used seventeen times throughout the Gospels and Acts but nowhere else in the New Testament. Nazareth is a small town in the region of Galilee where Jesus was raised.

57. **Read Matthew 2:22–23. Note that "he" in these verses refers to Jesus' stepfather, Joseph. How did God guide Joseph to raise his family in Nazareth?**

____

____

58. **Read John 1:45–46. Nathaniel was implying by his question that the Messiah was unlikely to come from Nazareth. What was Philip's response?**

____

____

____

Rabbi

Rabbi means master or teacher. Jesus is called Rabbi nearly a dozen times in the Gospels.

59. **Read John 3:2 and Matthew 7:28–29. Describe the differences between Jesus and other Rabbis.**

____

____

____

High Priest

The priests and high priests of the Bible offered sacrifices to God to pay for their own sins as well as the people's sins (Hebrews 5:1). Since the priests were imperfect and sinful, their sacrifices were temporary and would only cover sin for a time. Sacrifices had to be repeated year after year. When Jesus sacrificed Himself on the cross for all mankind, He acted as both the High Priest and a sacrifice. In fact, He was the perfect and final sacrifice, and He ended the need for the sacrificial system. Jesus continues to be the High Priest in heaven on our behalf.

Scan this QR Code for further study on Genesis 14:18-20 Melchizedek and Jesus our High Priest from Calvary Castle Rock

60. **Read Hebrews 10:10–14. What are some differences between the priestly temple system and Jesus' sacrifice on the cross?**

____

____

____

61. **Psalm 110:4. How long will Jesus be the High Priest?**

____

____

____

62. **Read Hebrews 4:14–16. How does Jesus as High Priest impact your life today?**

____

____

____

My Servant

Isaiah 42:1–4 prophesied about YHWH's Servant, and Matthew 12:15–21 tells us that Jesus is the fulfillment of this prophecy.

63. **Read Matthew 20:28 and Luke 22:24–27. What do we learn about what Jesus came to do, and how do we follow His example?**

____

____

____

We see that Jesus' human titles identify Him either with His work (as the anointed Messiah), with His Jewish roots, or with us.

Salvation is available only through faith in Jesus Christ. He proclaimed, "I am the way, the truth, and the life. No one comes to the Father except through Me" (John 14:6). Jesus had to be both God and man. As God, Jesus could appease God's holiness. Jesus had the capability of dying since death is the penalty for being a sinner or substitute for sinners. As both God and man, Jesus is the perfect mediator between holy God and sinful man (1 Timothy 2:5).

64. **Read 2 Corinthians 5:14–15. Knowing that God became man and took on the penalty of your sin, what should your response be?**

____

____

____

Bridge

Jesus is God, the Son of God, and the anointed Messiah, or Christ. This required Him to become a man to accomplish His mission of providing salvation for mankind. Ever since He took on humanity, He is, and always will be, fully man and fully God. That makes Him the most unique person.

Jesus Is the Most Unique Person Ever!

There is no one in heaven who is like Jesus Christ. No other member of the Trinity is also a man. There is no one on Earth who is like Him. No son or daughter of Adam is also God. The merging of the eternal Son of God with His created human body is called The Hypostatic Union. This sounds fancy but it's a simple term. Hypostatic means "personal" or "person," so the hypostatic union is the personal union of Jesus' two natures. It describes how God the Son took on a sinless human nature yet remained fully God at the same time. Jesus always had been God (John 8:58; 10:30); however, at His conception, Jesus became a human being for the first time (John 1:14). This is the hypostatic union, where Jesus Christ is fully God and fully man, 100 percent God and 100 percent man. He is not 50 percent God and 50 percent human. That would imply that 50 percent of both natures were excluded from Him as a person. He did not give up any of His deity when He took on humanity, and 50 percent of His humanity was not held back when the two natures merged.

> The personal union of God and man in Jesus is the Hypostatic Union

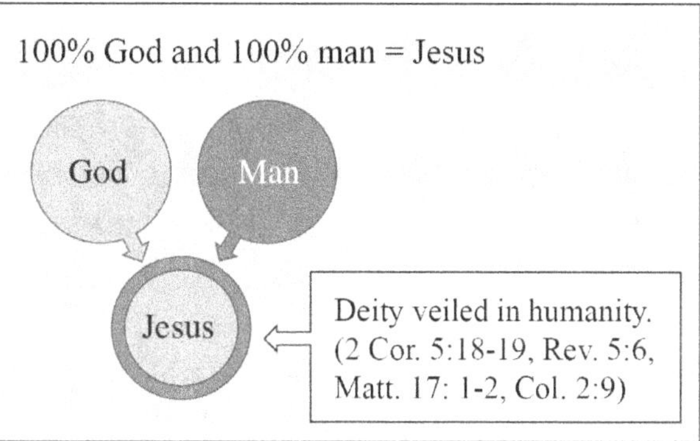

Two Natures Become One Person

Jesus was always mature in His deity. He did not grow His deity skills or attributes. They did not need to be tested or improved. He did not become more divine. His deity was always fully mature. However, His new humanity had to grow up. We see both great mysteries in Luke.

65. **Read Luke 2:46–52. At twelve years old, Jesus' deity leaps out at us as He is seen discussing theology with the Rabbis. How did they react?**

____

____

____

66. **What transition do we begin to see in Jesus' life in this passage?**

____

____

____

In these verses, we see His deity when He was discussing His Heavenly Father's business with the teachers and they were astonished (Luke 2:47). By contrast, Luke 2:51–52 says that He learned and grew into His humanity, because He was obedient to His parents and grew in wisdom and knowledge. The result was favor with God and man in both His divinity and His humanity.

Read Philippians 2:5–10.

When Jesus became a man, He did not give up His deity. Though He remained positionally equal with the Father and the Spirit, He chose to lay aside His privileges as God and humble Himself to become a bondservant in the exact likeness of men. As a child, Jesus submitted to His earthly authorities, His parents.

Read Matthew 3:13–17.

After His baptism, the Holy Spirit came upon Him, empowered Him, and led Him. As an adult, He submitted to the leading and guiding of the Holy Spirit. Jesus temporarily set aside using and publicizing His divine attributes so He could focus on doing the work the Father asked of Him. He trusted in His Heavenly Father and, by extension, the Holy Spirit for His entire ministry. He did this to be an example for us. We must learn to be dependent on the Father through the Holy Spirit, like Jesus was.

> Jesus was obedient and dependent on God the Father, through the Holy Spirit, to set an example for us.

67. **What is the Holy Spirit leading you to submit to today? What steps will you take?**

____

____

More About the Hypostatic Union

68. **Read the following verses and name the human and/or divine qualities or characteristics of Jesus in each passage.**

Matthew 8:23–27

____

____

Luke 4:2

____

____

John 4:6–26

____

____

Acts 17:30–31

____

____

Romans 9:5

____

____

The humanity of Christ is inseparable from His deity. Additionally, Jesus' humanity and divinity are not mixed but are united without the loss of separate identity. Jesus is only one person with one personality, not two. While the hypostatic union is understandable to a point, the depths are incomprehensible because it is impossible for us to fully understand how God works. As human beings with finite minds, we should not expect to totally comprehend an infinite God.

Summary and Transition to Chapter 3

We have examined the divinity and humanity of Jesus Christ, the only one who could accomplish the work of our salvation. In chapter 3 we will examine the reason why we needed the Son to be our sacrifice in the first place: sin.

Chapter 3:

Sin

This chapter will discuss the following topics:
Words for Sin
Origin of Sin
Consequences of Sin
Further Explanation of Sin Nature
Divine Judgment of Sin
Divine Cure for Sin
The Unforgivable Sin
End of Sin

First, we need an understanding of sin's origins, why sin was permitted, and why a believer in Jesus still sins. These are all crucial to comprehending why salvation is so necessary. The more we understand sin, the more grateful we will be for the cross of Jesus. The more grateful we are, the more we will love God.

1. **Read Luke 7:36–50. Was the sinful woman more or less grateful than Simon? How do you know?**

____

____

____

____

The more that we understand sin, the better equipped we will be to answer the "why" questions that people ask. For example, "Why is there evil and death in the world?" or "Why would a God of love allow sin to even exist?" Before answering these questions, we will first look at the words for sin in the Bible.

Words for Sin

The first and most basic word for sin, both in the Hebrew Old Testament and the Greek New Testament, means to fall short of perfection. **It means missing the mark, whether it is deliberate or not.** Not doing something we are supposed to do is just as much a sin as doing anything contrary to God's commands. We generally understand that wrong actions can be sins as well as wrong thoughts, attitudes, and desires. God revealed His laws through the Bible; therefore, we know what is expected of us. In the church age we are not under the laws of Moses, but we are under the laws of Christ as found in the New Testament.

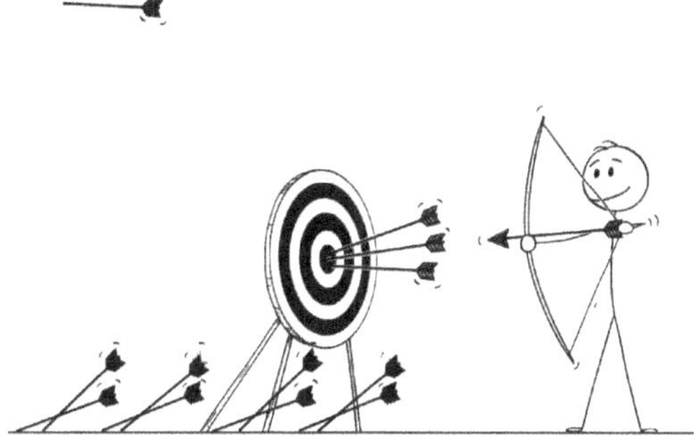

2. **Read Matthew 22:36–40. What is the revealed, perfect will of God that He has given to us?**

____

____

3. **Read John 14:15. How do we express our love to God?**

____

____

The commandments we are to keep as Christians are found in the letters of the New Testament, which include nine of the ten commandments given to Moses by God on Mount Sinai. We are no longer required to keep the fourth commandment about the Sabbath because our rest is now in Christ. We are called to gather in corporate worship (Hebrews 10:25), but it is no longer a specific day; we can gather any day of the week to worship. We demonstrate and live out our love for God and people when we keep and do His commandments. Failure to do so is a sin. The word *sin* also speaks of our sinful nature as well as our actions or inaction.

> When we keep God's commandments, we love Him and His people.

Words for Sin in the Bible

(in order from most to least frequently used)

Sin	Coming short of or falling from perfection	Isa. 59:1–2; Rom. 3:23; Rom. 5:12
Evil	Anything and everything that is in opposition to God	Gen. 6:5; Deut. 31:18; Isa. 5:20; Matt. 15:19
Iniquity	The intentional twisting of God's established reality by not receiving what God has clearly revealed about Himself, that He is the only God	Gen. 15:15; Ex. 20:4–5; Rom. 1:19–25
Unrighteousness	The evil deeds that result from iniquity	Rom 1:28–32; Gal. 5:19–20; 2 Pet. 2:12–15
Transgression	The deliberate overstepping of a boundary, the willful violation of specific commands of God	Lev. 6:2–3; Dan. 9:11; Matt. 15:2–6
Wickedness	The actions and expressions of the human heart in its depraved state	Gen. 6:5; Ps. 10:4; Matt. 15:15–20; Rom. 1:28–32
Disobedience	Choosing not to obey the truth as revealed by the Word of God	Deut. 28:15; Ezek. 5:7; Heb. 2:1–2
Lawlessness	Any action contrary to the law	1 John 3:4
Error	Knowingly acting against what is right	Isa. 32:6; 1 John 4:6
Unbelief	A lack of trust and faith in God	John 8:24; Heb. 3:12
Ungodliness	Lacking any fear of God	Isa. 32:6; Rom. 1:18–19
Spiritual Darkness	Rejection of the divine light of God	John 3:19–21; Acts 26:18; Eph. 6:12

4.   **The chart reflects the various ways the Bible identifies sin. Were any of these definitions new to you? If yes, explain.**

____

____

____

____

Bridge

Now understanding the words for sin, let's look at its origin.

Origin of Sin

One thing the Bible teaches in no uncertain terms is that God cannot sin; He is incapable of sinning. "This is the message which we have heard from Him and declare to you, that God is light and in Him is no darkness at all" (1 John 1:5). God is all-knowing, all the time, and nothing surprises Him, so the presence of sin was anticipated by God. Therefore, God provided a savior according to Revelation 13:8, "the Lamb slain [before] the foundation of the world."

Scripture states that sin did not originate with the first parents of all mankind, Adam and Eve; rather, sin originated with a created spiritual being whose name, before he sinned, was Lucifer.

5.   **Read Ezekiel 28:11–18. Describe Lucifer before he sinned and what happened to him.**

____

____

____

____

____

In Genesis 3, before Lucifer approached Eve to tempt her to sin, he had already sinned against God and was known by many names that reflected his fallen state.

6. **In Genesis 3, Lucifer was referred to as the serpent five times. Read Revelation 12:9. List the names that tie him to the serpent in the Garden of Eden.**

____

____

____

Before his fall, Satan was a beautiful creature made by God, but instead of giving God the glory, Satan took credit for his exalted status. We can't know exactly when Lucifer first sinned, but we know from Ezekiel 28 that he had already fallen before the garden. This chapter is a dual prophecy comparing the human Prince of Tyre with the Spiritual Being called the King of Tyre. The human ruler, the Prince, was prideful, and rather than recognize God's sovereignty, he attributed Tyre's riches to his own wisdom and strength. In verse 12, we learn that the prince is controlled by the King of Tyre, who, we are told, was present in Eden. Therefore, we know that the King is Lucifer and his pride had already caused him to sin prior to the Garden. Lucifer came to Eve as a serpent and deceived her by suggesting that God was keeping something good from both Adam and Eve. She took the fruit, ate it, and gave it to Adam, who willingly transgressed by eating it. Through Adam, sin entered the world and death followed (Romans 5:12).

Ezekiel describes this created spiritual being, but Isaiah 14 gives more specifics, including his name and descriptions of his sin.

7. **Read Isaiah 14:12–17. List the five "I will" statements of Lucifer's sin.**

    1. _______________________________________

    2. _______________________________________

    3. _______________________________________

    4. _______________________________________

    5. _______________________________________

8. **What one word would you use to describe his sin?**

Ezekiel and Isaiah talk about Lucifer's sin but not about why God allowed him to sin. Similarly, Genesis 3 tells us how Adam and Eve sinned and how she was deceived, but it does not tell us why God allowed Adam and Eve to sin. To understand why God allowed sin, we must look at the free will nature of both Adam and Eve and angelic beings.

God said, "Let Us make man in Our image, according to Our likeness" (Genesis 1:26). Since we are created in God's image and He has free will, then we also have free will. God allowed mankind to exercise free will when He commanded them not to eat of one particular tree among many other fruitful trees. They had a choice: either to obey by loving and worshiping God or to disobey and love and worship themselves. That same free will to choose was also given to Lucifer, since he was allowed to exercise the choice to rebel against God.

We must remember that God is good and can only be good. His ways are higher than our ways. God did not desire robots that worship and love Him, for robots cannot do either freely. Free will or choice makes all relationships meaningful. For example, if a married person takes their spouse and chains them to the stove and comes back every day and says, "Wow, my spouse really loves me! Look at how they are there waiting by the stove to make me a meal," this is forced slavery, not a meaningful or real relationship. However, if you return home and your spouse is there to greet you, of their own free will, this makes the relationship loving and valuable. God wants a real relationship with us, not robots with no ability to choose. That relationship would not be real or consensual. Free will implies the ability to choose something other than God's goodness.

> God did not make robots which are programmed to obey Him. He created people who can make the choice to follow Him. Choice brings value and meaning to our Godly relationship.

9. **Read 1 John 4:10 and verse 19. What does this say about God?**

The first human sin is the same nature as Lucifer's sin. Lucifer desired to be like the Most High God (Isaiah 14:13–14), and Adam and Eve likewise desired to know good and evil as God does. Lucifer's sin occurred right when He desired to be like the Most High God (Ezekiah 28:15–16). Adam and Eve sinned by eating the forbidden fruit, believing that they would become wise like God, knowing good and evil (Genesis 3:5–6).

10. **Read Genesis 3:1–5. What was the serpent offering Eve when she ate of the fruit?**

____

____

Understand that left to ourselves we would never naturally, in our fallen and sinful state, seek God. "There is none righteous, no, not one; there is none who understands; there is none who seeks after God" (Romans 3:10–11). However, because of God's love and desire for us to be in a relationship with Him, God awakens us to Him through His creation.

**Scan this QR Code for further study Calvary Castle
Rock Romans 1:18-23**

Consequences of Sin

Initial Consequence of Sin – Death

The first consequence of sin was and is death. However, there are four kinds of death. First is spiritual death, next a death that spreads to creation, then physical death, and finally the final death, which will come at the Great White Throne Judgment.

Spiritual Death

Spiritual death is separation from God. Sinful man can no longer be in fellowship with a Holy God. Eve ate from the Tree of the Knowledge of Good and Evil in direct disobedience to God and then gave it to Adam, who also ate. That day they both became corrupted with sin and died spiritually.

11. **Read Genesis 2:25. What was their state of mind before they sinned?**

____

____

12. **Read Genesis 3:6–10. What is the order of events immediately after they sinned, and what fundamental change occurred?**

____

____

This broken fellowship was pictured by Adam and Eve hiding from the presence of God in the garden. They knew they were guilty of disobeying God's command. They were ashamed and saw that they were naked and attempted to cover their nakedness with fig leaves. Something obviously was lost after their sin, and they suddenly noticed their nakedness. Romans 3:23 says, "All have sinned and fall short of the glory of God." At one time they were clothed in God's glory, which was removed after they sinned.

The fourth-century Syrian theologian Ephrem states in his commentary on Genesis 2:25, "It is because of the glory with which they were clothed that they were not ashamed. When it was taken away from them—after they had violated the commandment—they were indeed ashamed, because they were now naked." When God cried out in a broken-hearted manner, "Where are you, Adam?" it was the lament of a Father separated from His children.

> While sin and disobedience had not yet come on the scene, they were clad in that glory from above which caused them no shame. But after the breaking of the law, then entered the scene both shame and awareness of their nakedness.
>
> — John Chrysostom quoted in *Ancient Christian Commentary on Scripture: Old Testament* by Andrew Louth

13. **Read Genesis 3:21. What did God do to restore fellowship with Adam and Eve?**

This episode in the garden shows the first substitutionary atonement of something innocent dying for the guilty. Leviticus 17:11 says, "For the life of the flesh is in the blood, and I have given it to you upon the altar to make atonement for your souls; for it is the blood that makes atonement [covering] for the soul" (see also Hebrews 9:22). The covering of sins by animal sacrifice was temporary and would continue throughout the Old Testament until the final sacrifice of Jesus Christ.

Death Spread to All of Creation

When sin entered the world, all of creation was impacted, not just mankind.

14. **Read Genesis 3:17–19. How was the ground affected?**

15. **Read Romans 8:20–22. What is sin's impact on creation?**

Physical Death

Physical death is the separation of the body from soul and spirit. Adam died a physical death at the age of 930 years old (Genesis 5:5). The result of Adam and Eve's disobedience in the garden is that physical death is now the norm; our bodies begin dying from the moment of birth. Thus far, only Enoch and Elijah have escaped physical death; however, the saints taken at the rapture of the church will also escape physical death.

Scan this QR Code for further study
Doctrinal summary of the Body, Soul, and Spirit

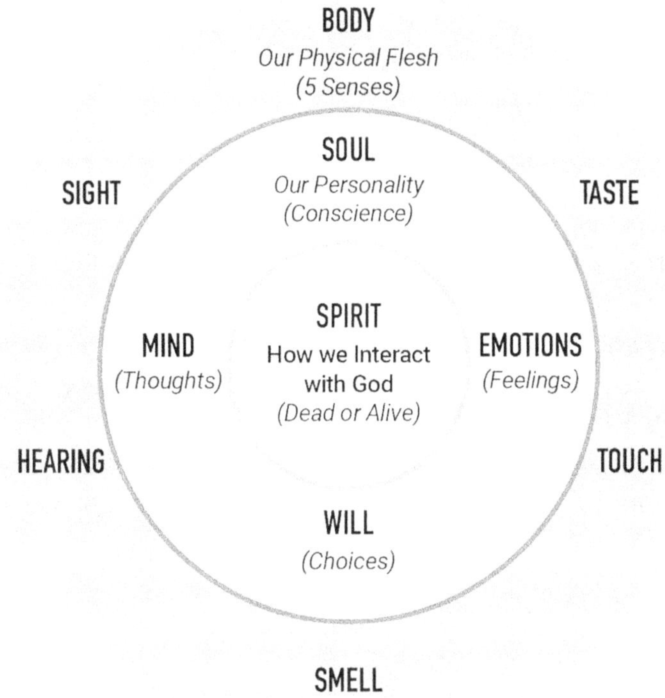

16. **Read Genesis 5. What is said about every one of Adam's descendants?**

____

____

____

____

Second, or Final, Death

Finally, the second death is the eternal separation from God forever. This occurs when a person dies physically without first receiving Jesus as their Savior. If Adam and Eve's sins had not been covered by God with the blood sacrifice, they would have experienced the second death (Revelation 2:11; 20:6; 20:14; 21:8).

Second Consequence of Sin – Inherited Sin Nature

The Bible tells us that all mankind is connected to Adam through his sin and death. Our sin nature is inherited from Adam.

17. **Read Romans 5:12. What do you learn about how sin entered the world and spread to all men?**

____

____

This may not seem fair to you, and you may be thinking that given the choice, you would have chosen not to sin. Romans 3:23 says, "All have sinned and fall short of the glory of God." This is evident in our own lives every day. Do we always love Jesus? Do we always love our brothers and sisters in Christ? Do we always obey God's commands every moment of every day in thought, attitude, and deed? No. Jesus died for us because we are incapable of saving ourselves. We are all born sinners.

> **Jesus died for us because we are incapable of saving ourselves.**

18. **Read Psalm 51:5. What does David say about himself?**

____

____

19. **Is this true of all humanity?**

____

____

Not only do we have the predisposition or inclination to sin, but we willingly and daily choose to sin. Willful sin is called transgression, and both the inclination to sin and transgressions have their roots in Adam. Through the first man, Adam, sin entered the world and infected all of mankind. We all became sinners through one man's disobedience. The good news is that through the Last Adam, one man provided forgiveness and righteousness to us through faith in His finished work on the cross.

20. **Read 1 Corinthians 15:45-47 and Romans 5:17-18. Who is the Last Adam and what do you learn about Him?**

____

____

Third Consequence of Sin – End of God's Rest and Start of Redemption

According to Genesis 2:2, God rested on the seventh day when creation was complete, and He would have remained at rest if not for sin. However, once Adam and Eve disobeyed God in the garden, His rest ended, and He began His work to save Adam and Eve and all mankind.

21. **Read Ephesians 1:4 and Galatians 4:4–5. When was God's plan of redemption formed? When was it implemented?**

____

____

22. **Read 1 Peter 1:18–19. With what are we redeemed?**

____

Additional Consequences of Sin

Sin caused the loss of God's glory.	Mankind fell short of the glory of God.	Gen. 3:7, Rom. 3:23
Sin is against God and separates us from Him.	Mankind needs reconciliation to God.	2 Cor. 5:17-20
Born spiritually dead.	Man needs to be born again.	John 3:5-16, Eph 2:1-9
Mankind is under bondage to sin.	Under the complete control of someone or something.	John 8:34, Rom. 6:16-22
Mankind commits personal sins.	Sin is an act of revolt against God.	Ps. 41:4, Eze. 18:20, Gal. 5:19-21

Further Explanation of Sin Nature

Other terms used for our sin nature are original sin, the flesh, or just the singular word: sin. It is called by some *original sin* because it originated on earth with Adam and Eve who then passed that sin nature on to all human beings through conception. It is also called *the flesh* because sin lives in our physical body. The Scriptures often use the word *sin* in the singular which speaks of our sinful nature as opposed to committing personal sins.

Scriptures that Speak of our Sin Nature

23. **Read 1 John 1:7-10. Summarize this passage.**

____

____

____

These verses make it clear that we all sin. Even though we are saved, all our lives we must answer for our sins by confessing them and trusting in His faithfulness and justice to forgive and cleanse us. We are called to ask forgiveness for the sins we have committed, but not for our sin nature.

24. **Read John 8:34-36 and Rom. 6:16-18. As believers are we slaves to our sin nature? Explain why or why not?**

____

____

____

____

25. **Read Mark 7:14–23. Describe the source of personal defilement.**

____

____

____

26. **Why does Jesus prioritize the inner person versus the outward behavior?**

Bridge

Can a holy, sinless God tolerate sin? NO! He must judge sin, but because He loves us, He also provides a way out by offering a divine cure for eternal condemnation.

Divine Judgment of Sin

The divine judgment for sin is death, as noted in Romans 6:23, "for the wages of sin is death." It is the penalty for being born a sinner and having a sin nature, which gives us the propensity to sin. This penalty applies to all human beings.

This judgment includes physical and spiritual death. Remember, there is also the second death, eternal separation from God, for those who have not placed their faith in Christ.

Divine Cure for Sin

Many people believe that good works are the cure for sin and can lead to salvation, but this belief is not supported in the Bible.

27. **Read Ephesians 2:8–10. How are we saved? What part do our works play?**

The faith spoken of above is faith in the blood sacrifice of Jesus Christ on the cross.

28. **Read Romans 5:8–9. What divine actions made this cure for sin possible?**

---

29. **Look up the following verses and record what it means when God takes away our sins. What happens to our sin?**

Psalm 103:12

Isaiah 38:17

Micah 7:19

Colossians 2:13–14

Hebrews 10:17

God has forgiven our sins! Therefore, we need to believe God over how we feel about our forgiveness.

30. **Read Ephesians 1:7 and Colossians 1:14. List the basis for our forgiveness.**

____

____

31. **Do feelings impact forgiveness at all?**

____

____

Read Luke 7:36–50 and notice the spiritual condition of the woman. Verse 37 says, "She was a sinner." The word _was_ is in the imperfect tense, meaning that she is forgiven and is no longer a practicing sinner.

Faith over Feelings! God has forgiven us even if we don't feel like it.

32. **What is this woman displaying by her actions in verses 37–38?**

____

____

33. **What point is Jesus making in verses 39–47?**

____

____

34. **What is Jesus trying to show Simon the Pharisee about himself?**

____

____

35. **The woman was already saved; she came back to Jesus to show her love. Jesus uses her testimony as an opportunity to show the Pharisees the way of salvation that leads to peace. What is the way of salvation?**

____

____

36. **Examine your own life. Are you more like the woman or the Pharisee? What would those closest to you say?**

Bridge

If our sins are forgiven forever through Jesus, then what is the blasphemy of the Spirit and why is it the unforgivable sin?

The Unforgivable Sin

To blaspheme, according to the Bible, is to speak against God in an irreverent manner. In Matthew 12:31 and Mark 3:29, Jesus declares that anyone who blasphemes against the Holy Spirit will not be forgiven and this blasphemy is subject to eternal judgment.

The biblical context of the mention of the unforgivable sin is that Jesus has just cast out a deaf and dumb spirit, which is a Messianic Miracle. The Pharisees could not deny that a deaf and dumb spirit had come out of the man. They either had to admit Jesus was the Messiah based on irrefutable evidence or come up with some other explanation. They not only denied that the Holy Spirit did it, but they went so far as to say that a stronger evil spirit cast out a lesser evil spirit. Matthew 12:24 says, "Now when the Pharisees heard it, they said, 'This fellow does not cast out demons except by Beelzebub, the ruler of the demons.'" The way Mark 3:30 puts it, "they said, 'He [Jesus] has an unclean spirit.'"

In Matthew 12:28 Jesus claimed to cast out demons by the Spirit of God, the same Spirit by which the sons of the Pharisees cast out demons according to Matthew 12:27. In other words, the Pharisees accused Jesus of casting out the demon by an evil spirit, Beelzebub, the ruler of the demons (Mark 3:22; Matthew 12:24), meaning they were accusing the Holy Spirit of being demonic. This was blasphemy and unforgivable.

This specific sin of blasphemy against the Holy Spirit was unique, and it will never happen again. To repeat it would require the same exact circumstances of Jesus' day, including Jesus being physically present on Earth, doing the same type of miracle in front of Jewish religious leaders, who would accuse Him of doing this miracle by the power of Satan. Replication of these circumstances is impossible because of the past death, resurrection, and ascension of Jesus. This sin of blasphemy, by some of the leadership in Israel against the Holy Spirit, cannot be repeated.

Jesus says in Matthew 12:32, "Anyone who speaks against the Son of Man, it will be forgiven him." Men speak against Jesus all the time; this is still forgivable.

Are There Any Unforgivable Sins Today?

All sins that people commit are forgivable, except the sin of unbelief. Not believing in Jesus as your Savior, by the time you die, is unforgivable and deserving of eternal separation from God. Besides the one-time blasphemy of the Holy Spirit committed by the Jewish religious leaders in Jesus' day, are there any other sins committed yesterday, today, or tomorrow that are unforgivable? Yes, there is one sin.

37. **Read John 16:8–9. The word** *sin* **is in the singular, meaning one sin. What is this sin?**

____

____

____

38. **Read John 3:16–18. What happens if a person dies without believing in Jesus?**

____

____

____

Bridge

After clarifying the many aspects of sin, we will close this chapter with the believer's responsibility regarding personal sin and the future joyful end of sin.

The Believer's Sins

At the time of the Apostle John, some teachers were suggesting that believers no longer have a sin nature and no longer sin.

39. **Read 1 John 1:5–10. Darkness refers to sin. What is the cause of broken fellowship with God?**

____

____

40. **What does it mean if a person says he has no sin nature (v. 8)?**

____

____

41. **Reread verse 9. How do we restore fellowship with God when we sin, and what is the result?**

____

____

42. **Are there sins that you need to take to the Lord and confess today?**

____

____

End of Sin

The Bible teaches that the day will come when believers have a final victory over all sin. This will occur either at physical death or at the Rapture of the church, whichever comes first.

43. **Read Romans 8:23. What are we waiting for?**

____

____

44. **Read 1 Corinthians 15:42–44. What happens to our bodies at the resurrection of the dead?**

45. **Read 1 Corinthians 15:54–57. What victory is ours at death?**

46. **Read 2 Corinthians 5:1–9. Here Paul calls our sin-natured bodies a burdensome tent. In contrast, he describes our permanent body as an eternal house made in the heavens. So, until we are clothed with our heavenly bodies, what should we be doing now?**

Summary and Transition to Chapter 4

Sin causes spiritual and physical death, affects all of creation, and results in eternal death for those who do not place their faith in Christ. Believers need divine help over sin to be able to live a life pleasing to our Heavenly Father. By the grace of God, through Christ's death, we have power available to us 24/7 for every sin that tempts us. But where does this power come from and how do we access it? In chapter 4, we will introduce God the Holy Spirit.

The Holy Spirit Is a Person

This chapter will discuss the following topics:
Procession of the Holy Spirit
The Holy Spirit Is a Person
The Spirit Has the Characteristics of a Person
The Holy Spirit Is God
Divine Attributes of the Holy Spirit
Types and Symbols of the Holy Spirit
Transcendence and Immanence of the Holy Spirit
The Holy Spirit Is Immanent (Within Creation)

Procession of the Holy Spirit

In the next two chapters we will focus on the most invisible (both literally and figuratively) member of the Trinity. We want to help clear the air about the Holy Spirit the person, His unique roles and His works, especially in our lives.

> The Holy Spirit gets a bad rap. He's often referred to as "It." He's mistaken for the force from Star Wars. He's confused with a ghost in paranormal activity. Oftentimes, He's just ignored or forgotten, and this makes sense since He is an invisible spirit. It can be hard to relate to Him and His work in our lives. You may know Him by name and know that He's mentioned during baptism but have no idea who He is, how He is at work in your life, or whether you should even care.

Let's agree this isn't a good thing.

—Jesse Wisnewski

The Holy Spirit Is a Person

Undoubtedly, the least understood person of the Godhead is the invisible Holy Spirit. *Spirit* seems a strange word to use for a person, yet a proper understanding of this person is basic to many doctrines—the inspiration of the Bible, aspects of our salvation, and many facets of the Christian life, just to name a few.

The Spirit Has the Characteristics of a Person

Normally when you think of what constitutes a person, you think of the material body and the immaterial soul, or spirit. Jesus was given a physical body because it was necessary to carry out His mission on Earth. The job of the Holy Spirit does not require a physical body, but He does possess the necessary immaterial characteristics of personhood: intelligence, emotions, and will.

1. **Read 1 Corinthians 2:10–11. What do you learn about the intelligence of the Holy Spirit?**

2. **Read Ephesians 4:30. What emotion is possible for the Spirit to experience?**

3. **Read 1 Corinthians 12:11. How does the Holy Spirit distribute spiritual gifts?**

In the three areas of intelligence, emotions, and will, the Spirit possesses the characteristics of a person.

The Spirit Acts Like a Person

Some actions of the Spirit distinguish Him as a separate personality and not, as some claim, merely a force that emanates from God.

4. **Read Romans 8:26–27. What does the Spirit do for us?**

---

5. **Read Acts 13:1–3. How do these verses show that the Holy Spirit acts like a person?**

The Grammar of Scripture Designates the Spirit as a Person

Proper grammar teaches that when a pronoun is substituted for a noun, it must be of the same gender as the noun, but this is not always the case when masculine pronouns are substituted for the neuter word *Spirit*.

6. **Read John 16:7–14. The personal pronouns Him, He, and His are masculine and refer to the Holy Spirit. How many times are these pronouns used of the Spirit in these verses? Why is this significant?**

---

7. **Read Ephesians 1:13–14. *Who* is a masculine pronoun, referring to a person. According to verse 13, who is the guarantee of our inheritance?**

____

____

____

____

These are examples of unusual grammar but excellent theology, because they show that the Spirit is not a neuter thing but a definite masculine person.

Bridge

The Holy Spirit Is God

The Holy Spirit is omniscient (all-knowing), omnipresent (present everywhere), and omnipotent (all-powerful).

8. **Read 1 Corinthians 2:10–12. What does the Spirit know about God the Father that no one else knows? How do these verses speak to omnipresence?**

____

____

____

9. **Read Psalm 139:7–10. Can a person ever get away from the Holy Spirit? How does this demonstrate omnipresence?**

____

____

____

10. **Read 1 Peter 3:18. How do these verses demonstrate the Holy Spirit's omnipotence?**

The Spirit Does Things Only God Can Do

11. **Read John 3:3–6. What is the Spirit's role in causing a person to be born again?**

---

12. **Read Matthew 1:20 and Luke 1:35. What all-important part did the Spirit play in the conception of Jesus?**

---

13. **Read Psalm 104:1–30. Who was instrumental in the creation of the world, according to verse 30 in particular?**

The Spirit Is YHWH

There are passages in the Old Testament that record YHWH (written as LORD in small caps) saying something, and then later the same passage is quoted in the New Testament attributing the Spirit as the speaker. That clearly tells us that the Spirit is YHWH, is equal to the other persons of the Trinity, and is therefore fully God. This is one of the strongest proofs of the deity of the Holy Spirit.

14. **Read Jeremiah 31:31–34. Four times the passage repeats the phrase "says the LORD" (i.e., YHWH). Now read Hebrews 10:15–17. To whom does the author attribute the Jeremiah quote?**

Divine Attributes of the Holy Spirit

Title	Description	Verses
Eternal	He has always existed.	Heb. 9:14
Omnipotent	The immeasurable power that can raise the dead is attributed to the Holy Spirit.	1 Pet. 3:18; Rom. 8:11
Omnipresent	He has always been present in the whole of creation.	Ps. 139:7–10
Omniscient	The Spirit knows all things.	1 Cor. 2:10–11
Love	The attribute of love belongs to the Holy Spirit to the degree of infinity.	Rom. 15.20; Gal. 5:22
Truth	As Jesus is the Truth in John 14:6, so the Spirit is the Truth.	John 14:17; 15:26; 1 John 5:6
Holy	To be holy is to be set apart; to be without flaw, blemish, or stain; and to shine with a fire-like brightness, full of glory and awe.	Matt. 28:19; Rom. 1:4

15. **Read Acts 5:1–4. What do you learn about the divinity of the Holy Spirit?**

Eternal

Hebrews 9:14 refers to "Christ, who through the eternal Spirit offered himself without spot to God." Here, all three Persons of the Godhead are named. The Son is offering Himself; the Father is receiving; and all is executed by the eternal Spirit. The term *eternal* here is assigned to the Holy Spirit. Since God alone is eternal, the Spirit is to be understood to be God.

Omnipotent

First Peter 3:18 reads, "For Christ also suffered once for sins, the just for the unjust, that He might bring us to God, being put to death in the flesh but made alive by the Spirit." In this passage the resurrection of Christ is credited to the energizing power of the Holy Spirit. In truth, all the works of the Spirit, as will yet be indicated, are works that demand divine omnipotence.

16. **Read Acts 2:32, Galatians 1:1, and John 10:18. Who else has the power to raise Jesus from the dead?**

____

____

____

Omnipresent

In Psalm 139:7–10 David says, "Where can I go from Your Spirit? Or where can I flee from Your presence? If I ascend into heaven, You are there; if I make my bed in hell, behold, You are there. If I take the wings of the morning, and dwell in the uttermost parts of the sea, even there Your hand shall lead me, and Your right hand shall hold me."

Spirit in this passage refers to the Holy Spirit. He is omnipresent. He has always been present in the whole of creation. Since the resurrection of Jesus, the Father, and the Son have been seated in Heaven (Acts 2:33–34), but the Spirit remains in the world.

Omniscient

According to 1 Corinthians 2:10–11, "God has revealed to us [the things prepared for us] through His Spirit. For the Spirit searches all things, yes, the deep things of God. For what man knows the things of a man except the spirit of the man which is in him? Even so no one knows the things of God except the Spirit of God."

Nothing is ever hidden from the searching discernment of the Holy Spirit, not even "the deep things of God." The text declares that, unaided, man cannot know the things of God (1 Corinthians 2:14). God is much more complex than we can comprehend. Since only the Holy Spirit knows and understands the deep things of God that are hidden from us, it is reasonable to conclude that the Spirit knows all things.

Love

Galatians 5:22 tells us, "The fruit of the Spirit is love." Therefore, the attribute of love belongs to the Holy Spirit. He is the source of divine love on Earth while the Father and the Son are seated in heaven. He fills us with the full measure of God's love to His children and through us to the world.

Truth

John 14:6 explains that Jesus is the Truth and we know that Jesus is the Truth, but 1 John 5:6 also explains that "it is the Spirit that bears witness, because the Spirit is truth." In the Greek text there is a definite article the before the word *truth*, so a better translation would be "the Spirit is the truth." The same situation is found in John 14:17 and 15:26. All three verses imply that the Holy Spirit is not just the Truth but the only source of truth. A prime example is His divine authorship of the infallible Scriptures (2 Timothy 3:16; 2 Peter 1:21).

17. **In the light of the Holy Spirit being "the Truth," how should we interpret the current sayings people use referring to "my truth" and "your truth"?**

Holy

"Go therefore and make disciples of all the nations, baptizing them in the name of the Father and of the Son and of the Holy Spirit" (Matthew 28:19).

He is called the Holy Spirit nearly one hundred times in the Bible, predominantly in the New Testament. Holy emphasizes His purity and sanctity but does not suggest that He is holier than the other two members of the Trinity. His holiness is not tarnished or diminished by the evil He suppresses in the world, nor by the resident evil of the believer's sin nature in whom He dwells. The primary work of the Holy Spirit through the sanctification process in the Church Age is to make holy those who come to Christ through faith.

Bridge

We have established the personhood and divinity of the invisible Holy Spirit. Types and symbols are used in the Scriptures to help us picture who He is and what He does.

Types and Symbols of the Holy Spirit

Symbols and Types are common figures of speech used in the Scriptures to convey spiritual truths. Symbols may be objects, actions, or creatures. Two examples include rocks as a symbol of stability (Psalm 18:2) and thirst as a symbol of spiritual need (Psalm 63:1). Some suggest there are hundreds of different symbols in the Old and New Testaments. Types are a particular kind of symbolism. They refer to a person, thing, or event in the Old Testament that is fulfilled or explained in another Scripture. They are usually fulfilled by the person or work of Jesus Christ or by the person or work of the Holy Spirit. Below is a list of the major symbols and types of God the Holy Spirit, which picture who He is and what He does.

Symbol/Type	Explanation	Verses
Oil	As oil is used for healing, illumination, and anointing, so the Spirit heals, illuminates, and anoints.	Ex. 25:6; 29:7; 1 Sam. 16:13; Luke 4:1, 18; James 5:14–15
Water	As water is poured out, so is the Spirit poured out.	Isa. 44:3; Acts 2:17; Joel 2:29
Fire	As fire consumes and purifies, so too the Spirit cleanses and refines believers.	Rev. 4:5
Breath or Wind	As the breath or wind blows where they wish, so does the Spirit.	John 3:8; 20:22
Dove	As a dove symbolizes innocence, so the Spirit confirms Jesus' innocence and holiness.	Luke 3:22; John 1:32
Guarantee	As a guarantee pledges the future completion of a transaction, so the Spirit guarantees the future of the believer with Christ in heaven.	Eph. 1:13–14

Symbol/Type	Explanation	Verses
Seal	As a seal signifies ownership, so the Spirit's invisible seal on believers declares to the spirit world that we belong to Christ.	Eph. 4:30; 1:13; 2 Cor. 1:21–22
Abraham's Servant	The Spirit is pictured as Abraham's servant who seeks a bride for his master. His name is Eliezer, which means the God of help or helper.	Gen. 24:1–67; John 14:26
Finger	At times the Spirit is the finger who is powerful and used by God; He is the finger who writes.	Ex. 8:19; 31:18; Luke 11:20; Dan. 5:5
Wine	One aspect of the fruit of the Spirit is joy. Wine is spoken of as making glad the heart. Being filled with the Spirit is contrasted with being filled or drunk on wine.	Ps. 104:15; Eccl. 9:7; Isa. 24:11; Eph. 5:18

Oil (Type)

Lewis Sperry Chafer writes extensively about oil as a type of the Holy Spirit. One fascinating example is found in the meal offering of Leviticus 2:1–16. Here, Christ is foreshadowed in His human perfections; oil appears, first mingled with the fine flour and then poured upon it. All this is a type that anticipates the life and ministry of Christ and His unique relationship to the Holy Spirit, which He maintained while here on Earth. Through this relationship Christ's humanity was sustained and His actions were empowered by the Holy Spirit. It was altogether possible, and it would have been natural, for Jesus to have sustained His humanity by the power of His own Deity. However, Christ is God's ideal man and the pattern for us to follow, so it was required that Jesus would call upon the Holy Spirit respecting every need and limitation that His humanity presented. So, too, man must be sustained by the Holy Spirit. In type (Leviticus 2:4–5, 7) the fine flour is mingled with oil, suggesting that, with regard to His humanity, Christ's body was generated by the Holy Spirit; and again (Leviticus 2:1, 6, 15), the oil poured over the meal foresees the Spirit coming upon Christ, as was true at His baptism.

Chafer explains that as oil was used for healing, for illumination, and for anointing for specific purposes, so, too, the Holy Spirit heals, illuminates, and anoints for specific purposes. Let's look at a few examples of oil as a type of the working of the Holy Spirit in several of these areas.

Healing: There was significance in the specific requirement for how a priest applies oil when cleansing the leper (Leviticus 14:10–32). The work of Christ in physical healing, as in spiritual transformation, was wrought by the power of the Holy Spirit. The cleansing of the leper is one of the most evident types of Christ since it previews salvation from sin.

Illumination: An equally beautiful type of the Holy Spirit is to be seen in the fact that oil served as the source of light in the Old Testament. The Israelites were directed to provide oil for the lights in the tabernacle (Exodus 25:6). Two vital truths are implied in this particular typology— namely, that God the Holy Spirit is the essential light and the believer is to walk in the light shed by the Holy Spirit upon his mind and heart, and that by so doing believers are themselves "lights in the world" (Matthew 5:14–16; Philippians 2:15; 1 John 1:7).

Anointing: In the Old Testament, kings and officers were anointed, indicating the direct authority of God over His people in that form of government. The connection between oil as a type and the Spirit as the fulfillment of that type is found in 1 Samuel 16:13, which reads, "Then Samuel took the horn of oil and anointed him in the midst of his brothers; and the Spirit of the LORD came upon David from that day forward. So Samuel arose and went to Ramah." This connection opens the door to many passages that use oil as a type of the Holy Spirit. In the New Testament it is universally accepted when the Bible speaks about anointing that the anointing refers to oil and therefore the context will indicate when it is the Spirit (see Acts 10:38 and 1 John 2:27).

Water (Type)

As water is essential for cleansing, satisfying thirst, reviving the dry soul, and refreshing, so is the Spirit of God. The Bible often pictures water as a type of the multifaceted work of the Holy Spirit. The imagery of water highlights the Holy Spirit's role in bringing life, renewal, and sustenance to believers. The living water offered by Jesus underscores the Holy Spirit's essential and transformative presence in the life of God's people.

18. **Read John 7:37–39. How is the presence of the Holy Spirit evident in the life of the believer?**

Fire (Symbol)

John the Baptist referred to Jesus who would baptize in the future with the Holy Spirit and Fire (Matthew 3:11; Luke 3:16). This fire baptism by Jesus occurred on Pentecost after the cross, the resurrection, and the ascension: "Then there appeared to them divided tongues, as of fire, and one sat upon each of them. And they were all filled with the Holy Spirit . . ." (Acts 2:3–4). The Holy Spirit, pictured as fire, either consumes as in judgment or produces the purity of God in our lives for the purpose of good works (Titus 2:14). As the silversmith uses fire to cleanse the dross from the precious metal, so God uses the Spirit to remove our sin from us (Psalm 66:10; Proverbs 17:3). His fire cleanses and refines.

19. **Read Malachi 3:2–3 and 1 Peter 1:6–7. During the process of refining precious metals by fire, the refiner skims off the impurities of molten metal until he sees his reflection in the surface of the liquid metal. What is God's purpose for the refinement in 1 Peter 1:6–7?**

____

____

____

Breath or Wind (Symbol)

The Holy Spirit is pictured as the breath of God. When man was created, God breathed into the lifeless form the breath of life and man became a living soul (Genesis 2:7). After His resurrection, Christ breathed on His disciples and said, "Receive the Holy Spirit" (John 20:22). Second Timothy 3:16 tells us that the Scriptures are God-breathed. The Holy Spirit is also pictured as the wind. Christ compared the working of the Spirit to the wind when He said to Nicodemus, "The wind blows where it wishes, and you hear the sound of it, but cannot tell where it comes from and where it goes. So is everyone who is born of the Spirit" (John 3:8). In Acts 2:2 the Spirit came on Pentecost as wind, "And suddenly there came a sound from heaven, as of a rushing mighty wind, and it filled the whole house where they were sitting."

> In Genesis 2:7 the word life is plural in the Hebrew and should read, lives. Adam was given two lives, physical and spiritual. When Adam was told about the tree of the knowledge of good and evil, "In the day you eat of it you will surely die," when they ate of the fruit, they died spiritually.

Dove (Symbol)

The dove is a symbol of innocence. At Christ's baptism the Holy Spirit dwescended upon Him in a bodily shape like a dove (Matthew 10:16). Of this important moment in the life of Christ on Earth, John the Baptist declared in John 1:30–32, "This is He of whom I said, 'After me comes a Man who is preferred before me, for He was before me.' I did not know Him; but that He should be revealed to Israel, therefore I came baptizing with water.' . . . I saw the Spirit descending from heaven like a dove, and He remained upon Him." The form of the dove at Jesus' baptism signified that the Spirit was one of pure and holy innocence.

20. **Read Matthew 10:16 and Philippians 2:14–16. What does it mean to be harmless as a dove?**

____

____

____

Guarantee (Symbol)

Three times in the New Testament the Spirit is referred to as a guarantee regarding the future for believers in Christ (2 Corinthians 1:22; 2 Corinthians 5:5; Ephesians 1:13–14).

21. **Read 2 Corinthians 5:1–6 and Ephesians 1:14. What does the Spirit guarantee?**

____

____

____

Seal (Symbol)

The seal of the Holy Spirit serves as a form of identification and ownership. This invisible seal tells the invisible spirit world that we belong to Jesus Christ. It is not seen in the physical world but is clearly seen by the angelic realm. An expanded translation of Ephesians 1:13–14 reads, "In Him [Christ] you also trusted, after you heard the word of truth, [specifically] the gospel of your salvation; in whom also, having believed, you were [immediately] sealed with the Holy Spirit of promise, who is the guarantee of our inheritance until the redemption of the purchased possession, to the praise of His glory."

22. **Read Romans 8:9. How do you know you belong to God?**

____

____

Abraham's Servant (Type)

There remains one outstanding type of the Holy Spirit, which is presented in Genesis 24:1–67. It is the part of the trusted servant whom Abraham sent to secure a bride for Isaac. Just as no personal name is given in the Scriptures to the Holy Spirit, no name has been assigned to the servant in this chapter. Both are known only by a descriptive title. In other chapters we learn that his name was Eliezer, the steward of Abraham's household (Genesis 15:2). His name means "help" or "helper," which is who Jesus called the Holy Spirit in John 14:26. The servant in Genesis 24 is sent to a distant place to secure a bride for the son. Every step of this journey and all that was accomplished is a picture of the Holy Spirit's present mission in the world and the calling out of a Bride for Christ.

Lewis Sperry Chafer quotes Dr. George E. Guille, who published a pamphlet in 1914 entitled *Isaac and Rebekah*, in which he writes,

> Three persons are prominent in this twenty-fourth chapter of Genesis: a father, his son, and their servant. The father and son are hidden in the father's house in Canaan, while the servant journeys after the bride. Jesus even now is away in His Father's house preparing a place for the Bride that the Holy Spirit is finding . . .
>
> The Holy Spirit, who wooed and won you for Christ, is dwelling in your heart, and is leading the way to the true Isaac. And at each

step of the journey, He has a blessed ministry to perform. He would take the things of Christ and show them unto you."

He who is not seen, who has never been "made manifest" as was Christ—excepting as He was identified to John the Baptist by the symbolism of a bodily shape like a dove—is, nevertheless, presented under types and symbols or emblems to the end that He may become real to the child of God and that His many characteristics may be disclosed.

Bridge

While the Father and the Son are seated in Heaven, the Holy Spirit is simultaneously outside and among all creation. These two characteristics are called Transcendence and Immanence.

Transcendence and Immanence of the Holy Spirit

Transcendence and Immanence are two natural and complementary characteristics of God the Spirit. Each characteristic manifests a different relationship He has with His creation. God is both transcendent (outside and over His creation) and immanent (among His creation). This is distinct from pantheism, which believes God is in everything and everything is God. Deism is another unbiblical view that affirms God is transcendent but denies His involvement within creation. True divinity affirms that God the Holy Spirit is both transcendent and immanent.

God is outside of, over, and amongst His creation.

The Holy Spirit Is Transcendent (Outside His Creation)

23. **Read Genesis 1:1. In this verse, God, in Hebrew, is *Elohim*, which is a plural noun speaking of the Trinity. How does this show the Spirit as outside creation?**

The Holy Spirit Is Immanent (Within Creation)

24. **Read Psalm 139:7–12. How does this describe the presence of the Spirit?**

---

25. **Read 1 Corinthians 2:10–13. Describe what the Holy Spirit is doing on a daily basis.**

---

26. **Read 2 Corinthians 13:14. What intimacy does the Holy Spirit provide for us?**

---

27. **We have established the Spirit as God and as Transcendent and Immanent. Read 1 John 5:7–8. How do these verses speak of both the Transcendence and Immanence of the Spirit?**

Bridge

The Holy Spirit is God. His role in our salvation is directed by the Father and the Son from heaven. He is sent by the Father and the Son for their purposes and to bring glory to both. Nowhere in Scripture do we read that the Holy Spirit seeks glory for Himself. This sending forth of the Holy Spirit is called the Doctrine of Procession.

Procession of the Holy Spirit

There is an order in the Trinity, and each member has specific roles to carry out, especially regarding our salvation. The Father plans and sends out the other two members of the Godhead to execute those plans. The Son was sent to accomplish the means of salvation and returned to sit at the right hand of the Father. After Christ's ascension the Holy Spirit was sent to convict the world of unbelief in Jesus and to apply salvation to those who believe (John 16:7–9).

The procession of the Spirit from the Father and the Son is taught in John's Gospel.

28. **Read John 15:26. *Proceed* means to go forth from one's abode. Who proceeds from the Father?**

____

____

____

29. **Read John 16:7. Who sends the Holy Spirit to believers?**

____

____

Thus, the Holy Spirit proceeds from both the Father and the Son.

Procession does not mean that the sender is the creator of the Spirit, for the Holy Spirit is eternal, but it does signify that He is being sent for specific purposes. After Christ's ascension, the Spirit is the major divine worker in the salvation of mankind. The Spirit was intimately involved with the formation of the Church at Pentecost.

30. **Read Acts 2:1–12. How did the pouring forth of the Holy Spirit impact the disciples and the multitude at Pentecost?**

The Spirit is the perfect ambassador representing the Father and the Son.

34. **Read Galatians 4:6. How does Paul describe the Holy Spirit?**

31. **Read Romans 8:9. List the three titles for the Holy Spirit in this verse.**

Because the Spirit proceeds from the Father and the Son, His identity is like both Father and Son, yet He is a distinct person. Taking on the likeness and characteristics of another member of the Godhead is not new.

32. **Read John 14:7–9. Who represented the Father to Philip?**

The Spirit takes on the representation of God the Father and the Son in the lives of believers. He is fully within all who believe in Jesus everywhere in the world.

33. **Read 1 Corinthians 3:16 and 1 Corinthians 6:19. Where does the Spirit of God dwell?**

____

____

____

Summary and Transition to Chapter 5

Having established the personality and divinity of the Holy Spirit, we will now look at His roles in the Godhead: His work in general in the Old and New Testaments, His gifts for the Church, His work in the world, and His work in the Tribulation and the Millenium that are yet to come.

Chapter 5:

The Work of the Holy Spirit

This chapter will discuss the following topics:
The Holy Spirit's Unique Roles
Work of the Holy Spirit
Holy Spirit and the Unsaved in the Church Age
Holy Spirit During the Tribulation
Holy Spirit In the Millennial Kingdom

After finishing the work of salvation, Jesus ascended into Heaven and was seated at the right hand of the Father, fully man and fully God. The Father sits. The Son sits. Who in the Godhead is actively working in the Church age on Earth? That would be the omnipresent Holy Spirit, and His work is for the Church Age in which we live.

The Holy Spirit's Unique Roles

Role	Description	Verses
1. He created.	He executes the divine purpose.	Gen. 1:2; Ps. 33:6; 104:30
2. He strives with mankind to restrain sin.	He resists through our conscience, laws, government, but He will not always do so.	Gen. 6:3
3. He generated Christ's body.	He gave the eternal Son a human body.	Luke 1:35; Matt. 1:18; Rom. 1:3–4
4. He convicts mankind.	He convicts the world of sin, righteousness, and judgment.	John 16:7–15; Heb. 12:5

Role	Description	Verses
5. He is the revealer of truth.	He reveals truth, and some of what He revealed became inspired, written Scriptures.	John 16:13; 2 Pet. 1:20–21; 2 Tim. 3:16
6. He illuminates the Scriptures.	He opens our mind to understand the Scriptures.	1 Cor. 2:9–10
7. He regenerates believing sinners.	He imparts eternal life through regeneration.	Titus 3:5
8. He adds to the Body of Christ.	He uses the Church to share the gospel.	Acts 6:3–7; 13:2–5; 28:25–31
9. He baptizes believers into the Body of Christ.	He immerses believers into the Body of Christ.	1 Cor. 12:13; Gal. 3:27
10. He indwells believers.	He lives in each believer.	Rom. 8:11; 1 Cor. 3:16; 2 Cor. 1:21–22
11. He seals believers.	His seal is a mark of identity and ownership on believers.	Eph. 1:13; 4:30; 2 Tim. 2:19; 2 Cor. 1:21–22
12. He is our guarantee.	He is given as a guarantee of our inheritance.	2 Cor. 5:4–5; Eph. 1:13–14
13. He is the believer's Intercessor.	He prays to the Father on our behalf.	Rom. 8:26–27
14. He is the Sanctifier.	He sanctifies us positionally, progressively, and finally.	1 Cor. 6:10–11; 1 Thess. 4:3–8; Rom. 15:16
15. He is the spiritual gift giver to the church.	He gives gifts to the church for the edification of the saints.	1 Cor. 12:4, 7
16. He is the Living Water.	He flows out of the Spirit-filled believer.	John 7:37–39; Acts 4:27–31
17. He fills the believer.	Believers are to be constantly filled with the Holy Spirit.	Acts 2:4; 6:3; Eph. 5:18
18. He brings forth fruit.	He manifests His fruit in believers.	Eph. 5:9; Gal. 5:22–23
19. He is the Helper.	He aids, comforts, and helps us.	John 14:16–17, 26; Acts 9:31
20. He is the Teacher.	He teaches believers the content of Scripture.	John 14:26; 16:12–15; 1 Cor. 2:10–13; 1 John 2:27
21. He is the Anointing.	He anoints believers to impart discernment and knowledge and to establish us in Christ.	2 Cor. 1:21–22; 1 John 2:20, 27
22. He empowers.	He dispenses to believers the spiritual abilities to do His will.	Acts 1:8; Rom. 15:13, 19; Eph. 3:20; 2 Tim. 1:7; Phil. 2:12–13
23. He witnesses.	He is a witness to us and the world.	Acts 5:27–32; Rom. 8:16; 1 John 5:6–8
24. He restrains The Antichrist.	He restrains the manifestation of the Antichrist.	1 John 2:18; 2 Thess. 2:6–12

The Holy Spirit's Roles Explained

He Created

In Genesis 1:2 the Spirit of God hovered, moved with energy to do His work in creation. It is written in Psalm 33:6, "By the word of the Lᴏʀᴅ the heavens were made, and all the host of them by the breath [or Spirit] of His mouth." Likewise, Psalm 104:30 reads, "You send forth Your Spirit, they are created; and You renew the face of the earth." The Holy Spirit executes the divine purpose with the Father and the Son, as co-creators.

He Strives with Mankind

Early in Genesis, God routinely contended with sinful men. In their rebellion they went astray, pursuing fleshly lusts. Though God is long-suffering and merciful, He would not strive with them forever. Judgment came to them with Noah's flood.

1. **Read Genesis 6:1–8 and 7:1. How did God respond to this ongoing disobedience in verses 3 and 7?**

____

____

____

Today, the Holy Spirit strives or contends with the sinner. He works in believers to help us fight against our sinful nature.

2. **Read Galatians 5:16–17. Name the two opposing forces. How do you have victory over the flesh?**

____

____

____

He Generated Christ's Body

Christ has always been God throughout eternity, but when the Father sent Him to Earth to be the sacrifice for our sins, He needed a human body. His human conception occurred when the Holy Spirit overshadowed Mary. The Holy Spirit was responsible for generating Christ's body from Mary's egg. He kept any sinful influence of Mary's humanity from infecting the physical body of Jesus. Joseph was not involved in the process at all, thus keeping the human Jesus from receiving Adam's sinful nature. Jesus was conceived of a virgin and born sinless. His divinity and humanity are forever united and inseparable.

3. **Read Luke 1:35. In this verse what names or titles would Jesus be given because of the overshadowing work of the Holy Spirit when He implanted Mary's egg with God the Son?**

____

____

____

4. **Read Romans 1:3–4. How do these verses show the merging of the human and the divine into the one person, Jesus Christ?**

____

____

____

He Convicts Mankind

While restraining and striving against sin, the Holy Spirit is also convicting unsaved individuals. He is always with the unbeliever to persuade them and draw them to Jesus.

The Holy Spirit Convicts the Unsaved

While restraining and striving against sin, the Holy Spirit is also convicting unsaved individuals. He is always with the unbeliever to persuade them and draw them to Jesus.

Scan this QR Code for further study Calvary Castle Rock Hebrews 12:1-11

5. **Read John 16:7–11. In what three areas will the Holy Spirit convict the world?**

____

____

____

6. **Explain in your own words how the Holy Spirit has convicted you in one or all of these areas before you were saved.**

____

____

____

The Holy Spirit convicts unbelievers of the singular sin of not believing in Jesus. He also makes it clear that Jesus is the only righteous sacrifice for our sin. His ascension into heaven shows that God accepted His righteous sacrifice. The Holy Spirit works to convince unbelievers that on the cross Jesus was victorious and Satan was judged, so that we no longer have to be a slave to Satan. Jesus can now be our King, and we can serve Him.

The Holy Spirit Convicts the Saved

There is teaching circulating throughout Christendom called Hyper Grace. Part of the Hyper Grace movement says that Christians are no longer convicted of personal sins, and they do not need to confess their personal sins. This is a false teaching.

Where do the Scriptures teach that believers are convicted of sin?

Read Hebrews 12:5–6 and Revelation 3:19. *Rebuked* in the Greek means convict.

Who in the Godhead is doing the convicting?

The author of Hebrews is quoting from Proverbs 3:11 and Psalm 94:12, and the word LORD means YHWH. Since YHWH Jesus is now in heaven seated at the right hand of YHWH the Father, the LORD in Hebrews 12:5–6 is speaking of YHWH the Holy Spirit. He does the work of convicting on behalf of the Father and the Son here on Earth, rebuking or convicting us of sin. It is the Holy Spirit who carries out the convicting work that Jesus requires, as explained in Revelation 3:19.

7. **Read 1 John 1:9. Since the Spirit convicts us of sin, what should we do and what do we receive?**

____

____

____

Knowing 1 John 1:9 brings more understanding to the sidebar Jesus had with Peter at his foot washing.

8. **Read John 13:3–11. What did Jesus mean by being completely cleaned?**

____

____

9. **What did Jesus mean when He said, "He who is bathed needs only to [have his feet washed]" (v. 10)?**

____

____

____

Part *(meros, Greek):* part, share, allotment, meaning participation with. (John 13:8)

Jesus is not saying that God cannot use Christians with dirty feet or even non-Christians who are not bathed. This principle is made clear by the Lord in other passages (read Matthew 7:21–23). He can use anyone at any time.

10. **What did Jesus mean when He said, "If I do not wash you, you have no part with Me" (John 13:8)?**

____

____

____

He Is the Revealer of Truth

Revelation can be separate from the inspiration of Scripture, but there is no inspiration of Scripture without revelation from God.

Revelation

In the Old Testament God gave His message to mankind through prophets (Hebrews 1:1). The Holy Spirit was moving and guiding every prophet so that they communicated exactly what God wanted man to know. This is called revelation; however, not all revelations became inspired Scripture. For example, in Revelation 10:4 something was revealed to the Apostle John, but he was told not to write it down as inspired Scripture. Second Peter 1:21 tells of holy men in the Old Testament being moved by the Spirit, who gave them revelations that became inspired Scripture. Does God reveal truth and direction today to Christians that do not become inspired Scriptures? Yes! But that truth must always line up with the Word of God. He does this within the Church through gifts of the Holy Spirit, to edify the Body of Christ. (The revelation gifts, such as wisdom, knowledge, prophecy, and the discerning of spirits, will be discussed in the next book in the chapter regarding the Local Church.)

Inspiration

The revelations that lead to the inspiration of the Scriptures are one of the greatest of all the Spirit's undertakings. In the production of the written Word of God, the Spirit adds not only revealed content but the overriding divine will and inerrancy to the human author's writings. The original writings of the Scriptures are the inerrant Word of God. The Bible is the written masterwork of the Holy Spirit and is demonstrated by some key passages.

Inerrancy (noun): In its original manuscripts, the Scriptures contain no faults or mistakes and are incapable of being wrong.

Second Timothy 3:16–17 says, "All Scripture is given by inspiration of God." The phrase "given by inspiration of God" is one word in the Greek text, *theopneustos*, which literally means "God breathed." The Spirit of God is the breath of God (Job 33:4).

11. **What is the source of Scripture, and what is its purpose?**

____

____

____

____

Concerning the writing of the New Testament, Jesus promised that the Spirit would recall to the human authors' minds the things that He had taught them, and the Spirit would give them even more truth (John 14:26; 16:13). The Spirit was the superior author, guiding and guarding the revelation of the New Testament.

He Illuminates the Scriptures

Revelation is what God imparted to men, whether those words became inspired Scripture or not. The natural man does not understand the Word of God. The spiritual man or woman needs the Spirit to illuminate the Scriptures and open our mind to understand the Bible. He unveils the very written Word of God, which He inspired, and now He guides us to comprehend all its truths.

12. **Read 1 Corinthians 2:12–14. Describe who gives you knowledge or understanding of spiritual things. Who does not understand the things of the Spirit?**

____

____

____

____

13. **Read Psalm 119:18. How can you use this prayer in your devotional study time?**

____

____

____

He Regenerates Believing Sinners

God creates, or regenerates, a new person when they believe in Christ. Faith and regeneration are closely associated but distinct. Faith, or believing in the Gospel, is our responsibility through which God's regenerating grace is received. Regeneration is God's supernatural act of imparting in the believer a new eternal life. Faith and regeneration happen together and are simultaneous.

14. **Read John 3:1–8. Compare and contrast human birth with being born again by the Spirit.**

____

____

____

15. **Read Romans 10:17 and James 1:18. Explain the role that the Word of God has in our regeneration.**

____

____

____

He Adds to the Body of Christ

The Church, the Body of Christ, belongs to Jesus, and He is the Head. The Holy Spirit has formed, guided, and empowered the Church from the beginning. This formation began at Pentecost when the Jewish disciples of Jesus in Jerusalem were baptized with the Holy Spirit. These Jewish believers became the nucleus of the Church. Three thousand Jews were added to the Body of Christ that day as the Spirit moved among them.

16. **Read Acts 2:32–33. Who poured forth the Holy Spirit on the day of Pentecost?**

This outpouring of the Holy Spirit gave the Church, as a group, power to be witnesses of the Lord throughout the world.

17. **Read Acts 1:8. Where was the early Church supposed to witness? Today, where is your circle of influence for sharing the gospel?**

The goal of witnessing is to present the Gospel of Christ crucified to everyone in the world. Jesus said in Matthew 16:18 that He would build His church (singular). It was to include all ethnicities from all over the world—one universal church but with local congregations, united in Christ. The initial group at Pentecost was all Jews, but this was just the beginning. By Acts 8, the Samaritans were added to the Church. Peter and John laid hands on those new believers in Samaria, and they received the Holy Spirit just like the Jews. They now became a part of the one Body of Christ that began with Jews only. Then shortly after, in Acts 10, the Gentiles were added through Peter. The Spirit fell on them just as He did at Pentecost, making the Jewish disciples realize that God's criteria was not based on ethnicity but on faith in Christ crucified. One church had been formed, including Jews, Samaritans, and Gentiles, through one baptism by Jesus. The Holy Spirit formed one ethnically inclusive, universal Body of Christ. That body is now being filled with believers from all over the world.

He Baptizes Believers into the Body of Christ

The Spirit's baptism of the believer into the Body of Christ means we are placed into Christ. This is not to be confused with water baptism or spectacular displays of power through the Spirit.

The Holy Spirit baptizes all believers into the Body of Christ. This is a one-way baptism into Christ, and there is no coming out of the Body of Christ, unlike when we come out of water baptism. The phrase "in Christ" is used eighty-six times in the Epistles. Being "in Christ" is an exclusive position of the Church and did not begin until the ascended Jesus poured out His Spirit on the day of Pentecost. Baptism by the Holy Spirit is something distinct to the Church Age. The baptism by the Spirit into Christ's body is foundational to all Christian growth, experience, and witnessing (Acts 1:8).

18. **Read 2 Corinthians 5:17. What changes occur when we are "in Christ"?**

____

____

____

He Indwells Believers

Unbelievers do not have the Spirit in them, but the Holy Spirit works alongside them to draw them to Christ. However, the Holy Spirit permanently indwells every believer at the moment of salvation.

19. **Read 1 Corinthians 3:16. What fact is stated here?**

____

____

____

20. **Read Romans 8:11. What is one benefit of the Spirit dwelling in us?**

____

____

____

He Seals Believers

God puts His seal or mark of identity and ownership on believers. According to Ephesians 1:13–14, we are sealed with the invisible Holy Spirit of promise. Therefore, the seal is invisible to men and not useful as such in the human realm. Because it is a spiritual seal, it would be visible only in the spirit realm. In the Roman world a seal was a mark of authority and showed ownership. Jesus' tomb was visibly sealed, which basically meant that all people should stop, stay away, and not break the seal by order of Rome. Since Christians are sealed by the Holy Spirit, they cannot be demon possessed. The fallen spirit world cannot gain entry because Christians are God's property. The Seal of the Spirit is a distinguishing identification and mark of divine ownership by God. We are under the seal of God's ownership and cannot be owned or possessed by another.

21. **Read 2 Timothy 2:19. What does the seal on God's foundation indicate?**

____

____

____

The Sealing of the Holy Spirit is not temporary, and it does not come and go. The seal speaks of a completed undertaking. The one who does the sealing becomes responsible for the person who is the sealed.

22. **Read Ephesians 4:30. For what future day have we been sealed?**

____

____

____

He Is Our Guarantee

When we are saved, we are sealed and indwelled by the Holy Spirit who anoints, sanctifies, and blesses us for the rest of our lives. We are also called children of God and heirs, joint heirs with Jesus Christ (Romans 8:17). This indwelling is a down payment or guarantee of the full inheritance to come in heaven. It is a promise of the heavenly glory that we will experience when we are with God for eternity.

23. **Read 2 Corinthians 5:4–5 and Ephesians 1:13–14. Who is the guarantee and what does He guarantee?**

____

____

____

____

He Is the Believer's Intercessor

The God who searches our hearts (1 Chronicles 28:9) is the same God who intercedes for us in the person of Jesus in heaven (John 17:20; Hebrews 7:25–27). The Holy Spirit also intercedes for us as we pray.

24. **Read Romans 8:26–27. There are times in your life when you receive devastating news or are so hurt that you just cannot pray with clarity. Explain how and why the Holy Spirit intercedes for us?**

____

____

____

____

He Is the Sanctifier

Sanctification is the process of being set apart and made useful for holy purposes. This ministry of the Spirit begins at salvation, continues throughout our earthly lives, and concludes when we are presented to God blameless in heaven (Ephesians 1:4; Jude 1:24). Sanctification is a threefold process that begins as positional, then becomes progressive, and ends with our final sanctification.

Before believing in Christ, we were positionally separated from God. Positional sanctification occurs when we believe in Christ for salvation and the Holy Spirit baptizes us into Christ's body. It is a one-time event that lasts forever. No classification known in heaven or on Earth is more distinctive, far-reaching, or true than what the Spirit completed when He positionally sanctified the individual believer "in Christ."

25. **Read 1 Corinthians 12:13 and Ephesians 2:4–6. When we are saved, where does the Holy Spirit place us?**

____

____

____

(Note: The Universal Church will be discussed at length in book two of the Rooted and Grounded series.)

Progressive sanctification is the work of the Holy Spirit to change us from the person we were before Christ, to the person God wants us to become in Christ. The power of the Spirit operates inside us to give us victory over our sinful nature. The Spirit works in us to be godly in character, in every attitude, and in all service.

26. **Read 1 Thessalonians 4:3–7. What is the will of God for you? What specific areas of sanctification are named?**

____

____

____

Final sanctification will be achieved when we are presented faultless before the presence of God in heaven, at the time of our death, or at the rapture. At that moment, we will be completely conformed to the image of Christ.

27. **Read Jude 1:24–25, 1 John 3:2, and Ephesians 1:4. In what condition will we stand before God in heaven?**

____

____

____

He Is the Spiritual Gift Giver to the Church

All spiritual gifts originate from the Father. James 1:17 says, "Every good gift and every perfect gift is from above, and comes down from the Father of lights, with whom there is no variation or shadow of turning."

Jesus said He would build His church (Matthew 16:18). Therefore, it is through the Son that the Father gives the one-time Foundational Gifts of being Apostles and Prophets and the ongoing Building Gifts of being evangelists and Pastors/Teachers (Ephesians 4:11). (These gifts will be discussed in more detail in chapter 8, "Church Foundations.") The Father, through the Holy Spirit, gives remaining gifts that edify the local church.

He Is the Living Water

In John 7:37–38, Jesus stood and cried out, saying, "If anyone thirsts, let him come to Me and drink. He who believes in Me, as the Scripture has said, out of his heart will flow rivers of living water." Living waters, like fast-moving mountain streams, are clean, refreshing and satisfying. When the Spirit not only dwells in us but also flows out of us, He affects our countenance, witness, words, and those around us as well (Acts 13:52).

28. **Read John 4:10–14. How do the natural waters differ from the living waters of Jesus?**

____

____

He Fills the Believer

The indwelling of the Holy Spirit is permanent, but the filling of the Spirit is to be repeated continuously, according to Ephesians 5:18: "And do not be drunk with wine, in which is dissipation; but be filled with the Spirit." The verb "be filled" is a command in the present tense, indicating that the filling is an ongoing, repeated, and requested experience. In other words, keep on being filled, for a Christian may be filled and filled and filled again. In Acts, we read nine times of disciples being filled with the Spirit. We should ask to be filled with the Spirit throughout each day and then believe that we are filled. It is not a feeling but a fact to be received and experienced by faith.

29. **Read Acts 4:27–31. What did they do after they were filled with the Holy Spirit? How does this apply to you?**

____

____

The comparison between drunkenness and being Spirit-filled provides the basic clue as to what it means to be filled with the Spirit. It is the idea of influence. Both the drunk and Spirit-filled persons are under the influence, whether alcohol or the Holy Spirit. They both do things that are unnatural to them. Believers, without exception, are expected to be constantly filled with the Spirit. This is not for a select few but a requirement for the normal Christian life.

He Brings Forth Fruit

All believers are to manifest the fruit of the Holy Spirit toward others to bring glory to God.

30. **Read Ephesians 5:9 and Galatians 5:22–23. How is the Spirit supposed to be manifested in our life?**

____

____

____

He Is the Helper

In the Upper Room Discourse (John 13–16), Jesus referred to the Holy Spirit as the Helper four times. *Helper* in these verses is the Greek word *paracletos*.

> Paracletos: (noun) helper, comforter, or advocate; one called to one's side as an all-sufficient aide; one who pleads another's cause as an intercessor.

31. **Read John 16:7. What needed to happen before the Helper would come?**

____

____

____

For three and a half years Christ had been the Paracletos to the disciples, their all-sufficient aide, helper, teacher, counselor, etc. Whatever

Jesus did for them and with them, the Holy Spirit would do after Jesus ascended. When leaving them, Jesus promised to send another Paracletos, or Helper, who was like Himself.

32. **Read John 14:16. *Another* in Greek is *allos*, meaning another like Himself. In this context, how is the Holy Spirit like Jesus? How long does the Helper abide with us?**

____

____

____

He Is the Teacher

One of the last promises the Lord made to His disciples before His crucifixion was that the Holy Spirit would teach them the many things they could not understand before His cross and resurrection.

33. **Read John 14:26. What does the Spirit do on behalf of Jesus?**

____

____

____

34. **Read John 16:12–15. What else does He reveal on behalf of Jesus?**

____

____

____

Our knowledge about Jesus comes from the written Word, the Bible. The Spirit must teach the believer the meaning of Scripture, including prophecy and those things that are hard to understand. He teaches us primarily through godly men (who teach men and women) and godly women (who teach women and children; see Titus 2:1–5 and 1 Timothy 2:12–14) who know and love the Word of God. He also directly teaches us through our own devotional and study times in the Word.

Read 1 John 2:18–27 with an emphasis on verse 27.

There are some who say that John's statement means that human teachers are unnecessary. However, in context John is reminding them about his previous teaching on antichrists who denied that Jesus came in the flesh (v. 22). John's point is that they do not need to be taught again about this subject because this truth is already abiding in them (v. 21). The Spirit will bring to mind all biblical truths that we have learned, whenever we need them. Being reminded is a great aspect of His teaching.

He Is the Anointing

The Anointing is the Holy Spirit who abides in us, and He is not limited to only ensuring that we are not deceived with regard to false teachings. The anointing Spirit recalls to our mind the correct teaching we have already received to distinguish it from the false. Jesus also received this same anointing Spirit to confront the false teachers of Israel, but more importantly, the Spirit enabled Him to carry out the Messianic missions of His first coming. The Old Testament records anointings with oil by judges, prophets, and priests on behalf of God for particular purposes. For example, Aaron was anointed with oil by Moses as High Priest in Exodus 29:7. David was anointed by Samuel with oil to be king in 1 Samuel 16:13. The anointing in both cases is with oil. As little Christs (Christians), we, too, have an anointing of the Spirit to be light and witness to the world and fulfill the callings and giftings that He has given through His Spirit.

In James 5:14, when James speaks of the New Testament, there is an anointing with oil by elders for those who are sick, who then pray that God would heal them of their sickness. The anointing in James 5 is with oil. The oil used in the James passage is a symbol of the Holy Spirit who heals. There are no other anointings with oil in the Epistles.

The anointing by the Holy Spirit is distinguished from anointings with oil and is spoken of in six verses in the New Testament: Luke 4:18, Acts 4:27, Acts 10:38, Hebrews 1:9, and 1 John 2:20, 27. All six verses involved a one-time act of being anointed with the Holy Spirit. The first four verses speak of Christ being anointed by the Spirit. The fifth and sixth verses of 1 John 2:20, 27 speak of our anointing once we are in Christ, for the purpose of being established in the faith. In verse 27, we read of the abiding Spirit within us. The significance of this abiding is, first, for the firm conviction of the truth of the gospel and God's Word, next, for learning more spiritual truth, and finally, for service.

Read 1 John 2:18–27 to answer the following questions.

35. **Who is being addressed in v. 18?**

____

____

____

36. **The Anointing has to do with whom? (v. 20)**

____

____

____

37. **What is the truth that they have been taught and are to have abide in them? (vv. 21–25)**

____

____

____

38. **Why is John writing to them, according to v. 26?**

____

____

____

Here is our expanded version of verse 27: "But the anointing which you have received from Him [the Father] abides in you, and you do not need that anyone teach you [about the truth that you have already been taught]; but as the same anointing teaches you concerning all things, and is true, and is not a lie [from deceivers], and just as it has [already] taught you, you will abide in Him."

Anointing, the Holy Spirit who abides in us, limited only to ensuring that we are not deceived? No. Jesus received His Anointing, by the same Spirit, to carry out the Messianic mission of His first coming. As Christians we too have an anointing to be a light and witness to the world and fulfill the callings and giftings that He has given us through His Spirit.

He Empowers

As believers we are not left on our own to follow the Lord. The Holy Spirit empowers us to work out the salvation we already have (Philippians 2:12–13). This means our salvation is to be seen by others as a witness for Christ.

39. **Read Philippians 2:12–16. How is your salvation to be seen by others?**

____

____

____

40. **Read 2 Timothy 1:7. What kind of spirit has God empowered in us?**

____

____

____

He Witnesses

The Holy Spirit Himself is a witness (Acts 5:32).

41. **Read Romans 8:14–17. To what does the Spirit bear witness?**

____

____

____

42. **Read 1 John 5:6–7. Of whom does the Spirit bear witness?**

____

____

____

He Restrains the Antichrist

> Let no one deceive you by any means; for that Day [the second coming of Christ] will not come unless the falling away comes first, and the man of sin is revealed, the son of perdition [two titles of the Antichrist], who opposes and exalts himself above all that is called [or described as] God or that is worshiped, so that he [the Antichrist] sits as God in the temple of God [in Jerusalem], showing himself that he is God. Do you not remember that when I was still with you, I told you these things? And now you know what is restraining, that he [the Antichrist] may be revealed in his own [appointed] time. For the mystery of lawlessness is already at work; only He [the Holy Spirit] who now restrains [the manifestation of the Antichrist] will do so until He [the Holy Spirit] is taken out of the way [not removed] from the earth, but He stops restraining the Antichrist]. (2 Thessalonians 2:3–7, expanded version)

"That the Holy Spirit within the church is the restrainer is supported by the fact that the restrainer is referenced both as a thing (the word *what* in verse 6 is in the neuter gender) and as a person (masculine gender "He" in verse 7). Angels such as Michael are never referred to in the neuter gender. Also, the power delaying Satan's masterplan to unveil his false messiah must be of God. It makes much more sense to say that the Holy Spirit is curbing the devil than a political entity or even an angel. The Holy Spirit of God is the only person with sufficient supernatural power to do this restraining" (https://www.gotquestions.org/restrainer.html).

Summary of the Holy Unique Roles

The Holy Spirit has unique roles within the Godhead. He is the power and executor behind the Father and the Son's creation. He is uniquely involved with all of mankind striving against sin, convicting the world of sin, and restraining the manifestation of the Antichrist. He has the divine responsibility for everything concerning the Word of God. He conceived the sinless body of Jesus in the womb of Mary. He was the power of Jesus when He was on Earth. Through the eternal Spirit, Jesus was offered to the Father in sacrifice. He applies the Word of God and the finished work of Christ to all who believe. He formed and filled the one Church, the one Body of Christ. He is the Spirit of Christ to the Church and all that the Church needs to be a light and witness in the world. For believers He is the helper, the giver of spiritual gifts, the anointing, and the one who establishes us in the faith. He lives in those who put their faith in Christ crucified, and He is called holy because He is sinless and makes holy those in whom He resides.

Work of the Holy Spirit

Having looked at the Holy Spirit's credentials as God and the broad spectrum of His many unique roles within the Godhead, we will now look at His unique work with believers in both the Old and New Testaments: His works and gifts within the Church, His convicting work toward an unbelieving world, His work during the Great Tribulation, and finally the Kingdom Age.

Old Testament Believers

The Holy Spirit selectively, though not always permanently, indwelled some believers in the Old Testament.

43. **Read Genesis 41:38, Exodus 31:1–5, Numbers 27:18, and Daniel 4:8. Who are some of God's people whom the Spirit indwelled in the Old Testament?**

____

____

Nehemiah 9:30 reads, "Yet for many years You had patience with them, and testified against them by your Spirit in Your prophets." Here, the Spirit is in the prophets. In Scripture there are also female prophets, called prophetesses.

44. **Read Exodus 15:20, Judges 4:4, and 2 Chronicles 34:22. List some of these female prophetesses.**

____

____

The Holy Spirit also sometimes came <u>**upon**</u> Old Testament people.

45. **Read Judges 3:9–10, Judges 13:24–25, and 1 Samuel 11:6. Where is the Spirit in these passages?**

____

____

In the Old Testament, the Spirit could depart from men after coming upon them.

46. **Read Judges 16:20 and 1 Samuel 16:14. From whom did the Holy Spirit depart in these verses?**

____

____

In the Old Testament, the permanency and indwelling of the Spirit in believers was not guaranteed. In the New Testament, after Christ ascended into Heaven, believers are promised the permanent indwelling of the Holy Spirit.

47. **Read Psalm 51:11. What was David's concern?**

____

____

The Holy Spirit can also influence people. Consider the following verse: "And so we have the prophetic word confirmed, which you do well to heed as a light that shines in a dark place, until the day dawns and the morning star rises in your hearts; knowing this first, that no prophecy of Scripture is of any private interpretation, for prophecy never came by the will of man, but holy men of God spoke as they were moved by the Holy Spirit" (2 Peter 1:19–21).

In the phrase "**moved** by the Holy Spirit," the word _by_ in Greek is _hupo_, meaning under—in other words, "under the influence." So this verse is saying that "holy men of God spoke as they were **moved** [or influenced] by the Holy Spirit."

New Testament Believers

At Pentecost a change occurred when the Holy Spirit began to permanently indwell all believers. This permanent indwelling is possible because our sins and bondage to our sin nature was dealt with at the cross of Jesus Christ.

48. **Read John 14:16–17. Describe our relationship with the Holy Spirit.**

____

____

He gives each of us one or more gifts to contribute to the proper functioning of the church. There are four main passages that speak of spiritual gifts: 1 Peter 4:10–11, Romans 12:4–8, Ephesians 4:11–16, and 1 Corinthians 12–14.

49. **Read 1 Peter 4:10–11. Why do we receive spiritual gifts?**

____

____

Holy Spirit and the Unsaved in the Church Age

Convicting Unbelievers

The Holy Spirit strives against sin and restrains the manifestation of the evil one. He convicts unsaved people of the truth of the gospel, and it's up to the unsaved person to believe. Conviction is making the message clear, not the saving of the soul—that's regeneration through faith.

Read John 16:8–11. The Holy Spirit makes clear the truth about sin, righteousness, and judgment, as explained below:

- The Holy Spirit establishes that mankind is under condemnation because of sin, specifically because for those who do not believe in Jesus.
- The Holy Spirit proves the righteousness of Christ and the acceptance of Christ's sacrifice on the cross by His resurrection and His ascension into heaven.

- All the righteous claims of Jesus and His complete sacrifice for sins were fully vindicated when He returned to heaven. The proof of judgment to come is based on the judgment of Satan at the cross. In other words, if Satan has been judged (John 12:31), what chance can any unbeliever have of escaping judgment if he or she refuses the grace of God?

There is a logical order to the Spirit's work of conviction. First, people need to see their sinful state. Then, they need to have proof of the righteousness of the Savior who can save them and all people from sin. Finally, people need to be reminded that everyone who refuses to receive the Savior cannot be saved by any other means and will face certain condemnation and eternal judgment.

Holy Spirit During the Tribulation

Many expositors teach that the Holy Spirit will be removed from the earth during the seven-year tribulation. This is a misinterpretation of 2 Thessalonians 2:7, which reads, "For the mystery of lawlessness is already at work; only He who now restrains will do so until He is taken out of the way." The context of the verse is the Holy Spirit stepping back from restraining the evil one but not discontinuing all His other works. This permits the Antichrist to be revealed and manifested to the world. Evil will be rampant, though not unpunished, during the tribulation. The Holy Spirit will continue working with people to bring them to Christ.

50. **Read Revelation 7:9–14. What is the result of the Holy's Spirit's salvation work during the tribulation?**

____

____

51. **Read Revelation 6:9 and 7:9–14. What is the result of the Holy Spirit's salvation work during the tribulation?**

____

____

At the end of the Tribulation the Spirit will be poured out on the nation of Israel when they repent of their rejection of Jesus as their Messiah (Hosea 5:13–6:3), fulfilling the prophecy in Joel 2:28–32. This outpouring will set the stage for Jesus' return to the earth.

Holy Spirit in the Millennial Kingdom

After the Tribulation, there will be the thousand-year reign of Christ on Earth, called the Millennial Kingdom Age. During this time, little is specifically written about the Holy Spirit. However, the fullness of the Spirit on Christ the King will be evident (Isaiah 11:2–3). The salvation of Israel as a nation (Jeremiah 31:31–34; Romans 11:26) and the Spirit's indwelling of their lives (Ezekiel 36:26–27) will continue with them into the Kingdom Age.

Jesus died for all sins; therefore, the benefits of the cross through the Holy Spirit are the same in the Church Age, the Tribulation, and the Millennial Kingdom.

Summary and Transition to Chapter 6

We have discovered that the Holy Spirit is God, a Person, and always Spirit. He is transcendent (outside creation) and at the same time immanent (within all of creation), without being a part of it. We saw His submission to the Father and the Son when He proceeded from them to accomplish the work of redemption in mankind. He is the gift giver and administrator of those gifts for the church. He has unique roles convicting the unsaved of their sin of unbelief and restraining the evil one in the world. Next, we will learn about God the Father and His attributes.

Chapter 6:

God the Father

This chapter will discuss the following topics:
How God the Father Reveals Himself
Hebrew Names and Titles of God the Father
Compound Hebrew Names and Titles of God the Father
New Testament Greek Titles of God the Father
New Testament Descriptive Titles of God the Father
The Attributes of God

We live in the Church Age under the New Covenant, and we refer to the first person of the Godhead as Father. Father is a title, not a name, but we often treat titles like Father or Lord as names. The second person of the Godhead is referred to as the Son, and Jesus is His name. The third person of the Godhead, the Spirit, is commonly referred to as the Holy Spirit in the New Testament; we do not know His name, but we call Him by His descriptive title, Holy Spirit. In previous chapters we have focused on the Son and the Holy Spirit, and now we turn our focus on God the Father.

How God the Father Reveals Himself

Before there was a beginning, there was God. He created the heavens and the earth and then man and woman in His image and likeness. God also created language so that He could communicate with them and they with Him. His communications are often called revelations (Psalm 98:2; Amos 3:7), and some have become a permanent record, which is the Bible we have today. Through this Word we come to know God—His person, character, capabilities, and attributes. The Supreme Being and Creator of the universe has chosen to reveal Himself through His name, His descriptive titles for Himself, and His attributes. God has also revealed Himself through His Son, as discussed in chapter 2.

Hebrew Names and Titles of God the Father

Name	Description	Verses
YHWH (Yah-weh*)	I AM THAT I AM	Ex. 3:14–15; 20:7; Isa. 42:8; Jer. 33:2
El/Elohim (El-o-him)	Supernatural Being	Gen. 1:1; Job 1:1; Ps. 91:2
Adon/Adonai (Ad-o-nai)	Lord, Master	Gen. 15:2; Deut. 10:17; Josh. 5:14

YHWH

The most common name for God in the Hebrew Old Testament is comprised of four Hebrew letters that transliterate into the four English letters YHWH. This name of God is known as the Tetragrammaton, meaning the four letters, and is used over seven thousand times in the Old Testament. Exactly how this four-letter name was to be pronounced is no longer known because the Jewish people refused to pronounce this name of God, because they thought they were taking the name of the Lord God in vain. Some suggest that the pronunciation YHWH should be Yahweh. These four letters are translated into English Bibles as Lord (all capitalized) and also by the term God (all capitalized).

1. **Read Exodus 15:3, Isaiah 42:8, and Hosea 12:5. What is God's Name?**

2. **Read Exodus 5:1–2. How does Moses introduce God to Pharaoh?**

3. **Write down the two responses of Pharaoh using the name of God.**

The name YHWH also emphasizes three additional aspects of this name of God the Father:

- YHWH, the Covenant Keeper
- The exclusive nature of His name
- YHWH's hatred of sin

YHWH as the Covenant Keeper suggests that He is unchanging in His relationship to Israel. He will do everything He promises.

4. **Read Exodus 2:24, Psalm 89:34, Ezekiel 16:59–60. How do these verses collectively confirm YHWH's unchanging relationship with His people?**

____

____

____

Another emphasis of the name YHWH is the exclusive nature of His name, meaning that no other god has this name.

5. **Read Isaiah 44:6 and Isaiah 45:5–6. How do these verses emphasize YHWH's name?**

____

____

____

The name YHWH also points to God's hatred of sin and His work of redemption.

6. **Read Genesis 6:3–6 and Exodus 34:6–7. How do these passages speak to YHWH's hatred of sin?**

____

____

____

____

7. **Read Genesis 3:21, Exodus 12:12–14, Isaiah 53:6–7 and 10, and John 1:29. How do these passages demonstrate YHWH's work of redemption because of sin?**

____

____

____

El and Elohim

The second most common Hebrew name is a descriptive title. The singular form is El, but the most used is the plural Elohim. The plural form refers to supernatural beings, including angels and false gods, and is translated either for the true God (singular) or false gods (plural). This plural form is used over 2,500 times in the Old Testament, and the majority of the time it is used of the true God. There are some exceptions, but in those instances the context will make it clear if it is speaking of the true God or false gods.

The name or title El or Elohim has a threefold emphasis: God's power (Psalm 62:11), God's Creation (Genesis 1:1), and God's attributes (Psalm 86:15–17).

8. **Read Psalm 86:15–17. List His attributes.**

____

____

____

____

Adon and Adonai

The third most common Hebrew title for God is Adon and its plural form, Adonai. The root of the word *Adonai* means to judge or rule. It has three basic translations in English—lord, master, or owner—and can be used of God or man. When the word *Adonai* is used for God, then the translation has only the first letter capitalized: Lord. However, when used for man, it is not capitalized. The emphasis of Adonai (Lord) is that God is the Master Ruler to whom everyone and everything is or will be subject.

Compound Hebrew Names and Titles of God the Father

Name	Description	Verses
YHWH Elohim	Lᴏʀᴅ God (relationship of God to man)	Gen. 2:4–9; 2 Chron. 32:16–17
Adonai YHWH	God is the Covenant Keeper	Gen. 15:2; 2 Sam. 7:18–20; Isa. 7:7
YHWH Tzvaot (şă·vă·ot)	YHWH of Hosts, head of angelic armies	1 Kings 19:14; Isa. 1:9; 10:24–27; 31:4–5
YHWH Yireh (yrī·ăh)	YHWH sees and provides	Gen. 22:14
YHWH Rophecha (ră·fă)	YHWH, your Healer	Ex. 15:26
YHWH Nissi (nēs·sē)	YHWH, my Banner	Ex. 17:15
YHWH Mqaddis (kä·dawsh)	YHWH, your Sanctifier	Ex. 31:13; Lev. 20:7–8
YHWH Shalom (sha-lom)	YHWH is peace	Judg. 6:24
YHWH Ro'h (ra-ah)	YHWH, my Shepherd	Ps. 23:1
YHWH Tzidkeinu (sid-qe)	YHWH, our Righteousness	Jer. 23:6; 33:16
YHWH Makeh (me·ḵāh)	YHWH smites	Ezek. 7:9
El Shaddai (el sha-dai)	Almighty God	Gen. 17:1; 28:3; Ex. 6:3; Ezek. 10:5
El Elyon (ĕl el-yôn)	God Most High (above all)	2 Sam. 22:14–15; Ps. 57:2
El Olam (el o-lam)	The Everlasting God	Gen. 21:33; Isa. 40:28
El Ro'i (el rō)	The God who sees	Gen. 16:13
El Gmulot (găm·mă·lōt)	God of Recompense	Jer. 51:56

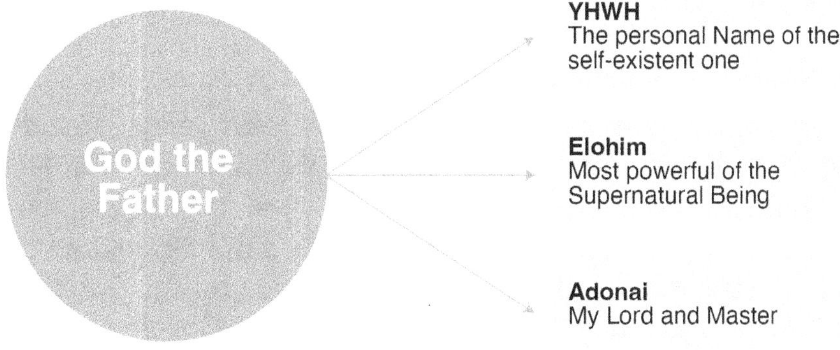

New Testament Greek Titles of God the Father

Name	Description	Verses
Theos (the-ŏs)	The true God	John 1:1
Kurios (kur-e-ōs)	The Lord Possessor and Ruler	Matt. 11:25; Acts 2:34; Rev. 4:8; 22:6
Pater (payter)	Father	Luke 11:1–2; John 20:17; Rom. 8:15; Gal. 4:6
Despoteis (des-pō-tes)	Lord, Master, Owner	Luke 2:29; Acts 4:24
Ktizo (k-tē-zō)	Creator	Rom. 1:25; 1 Pet. 4:19
Pantokrator (pan-tō-kra-tor)	The Almighty	2 Cor. 6:18; Rev. 21:22
Hupsistos (hoop-sis-tōs)	The Highest	Matt. 21:9

Theos

Theos is the Greek equivalent to the Hebrew title Elohim and is translated God. It expresses the essential deity and essence of God as seen in John 1:1. Like Elohim, it can be used for the heathen gods (Acts 28:6) and the Antichrist (2 Thes. 2:4). Context determines how it is translated.

Kurios

Kurios in the Greek is translated Lord and is the equivalent of and used for two Hebrew names and titles, YHWH and Adonai. The root for Kurios means power. It emphasizes God as the Mighty One, the Lord Possessor, and Ruler. It is used of both human (Matthew 6:24) and divine relationships (Ephesians 6:9).

Pater

Pater (Greek) is translated Abba (Aramaic) and Father, and Abba is an intimate word for Father. When the disciples asked Jesus, "Teach us to pray," Jesus said to them, "When you pray, say: Our Father in Heaven" (Luke 11:1–2). Jesus introduced the God of Israel to the disciples in the most intimate way. In human relationships only a man's children can address him as Father; so, too, only children of God can call God Father. In Romans Paul tells us that those who are in Christ are Children of God. This is why Paul goes on to say, "You received the Spirit of adoption by whom we cry out 'Abba, Father'" (Romans 8:15). Paul also says, "And because you are sons, God has sent forth the Spirit of His Son into your hearts, crying out, 'Abba, Father!'" (Galatians 4:6). When you receive Jesus, you become a child of God (John 1:12); thus, you get to have this amazing intimate relationship with God and call Him Father.

New Testament Descriptive Titles of God the Father

Name	Description	Verses
The Father	He is the Father of all believers in Christ.	Matt. 6:9; Rom. 8:15; Eph. 4:6
Father of Mercies and Comfort	He is the source of all mercies that brings comfort.	2 Cor. 1:3
Father of Glory	His divine splendor and perfection give us the Spirit of wisdom and revelation of Himself.	Eph. 1:17
Father of Lights	He is the source of illuminating truth where there is no deception.	James 1:17
Father of spirits	He is the Father of all spiritual beings.	Heb. 12:9

The Attributes of God

Since we have the benefit of the entire Bible, we can summarize His incomprehensible and comprehensible attributes. God revealed these attributes to mankind progressively over time. He did so through direct revelation to certain men who included His descriptive names. These revelations became inspired Scripture. Many of His names and titles reveal and describe His attributes.

God the Father's Incomprehensible Attributes

God's incomprehensible attributes are those that we as humans cannot fully understand. The six attributes, listed in the chart below, are exclusive to Him and cannot be personally experienced by people. Though we may grasp them in a limited way, we will never completely understand them. We should respond to these incomprehensible attributes with profound humility. What has been revealed is enough for us to be in awe of Him and to trust Him.

The secret things belong to the LORD our God, but those things which are revealed belong to us and to our children forever, that we may do all the words of this law.

— Deuteronomy 29:29

Incomprehensible Attributes	Verses
He is eternal.	Deut. 33:27; 2 Pet. 3:8
He is immense and omnipresent.	Jer. 23:23–24; Ps. 139:7–12
He is immutable.	Mal. 3:6; Heb. 6:17; James 1:17
He is independent.	Isa. 40:13–14; John 5:26; Acts 17:24–25
He is a self-existent Spirit.	John 4:24; Col. 1:15–16; 1 Tim. 1:17
He is unified.	Deut. 6:4; John 10:30; 1 John 5:7–8

He Is Eternal

God alone is eternal, meaning He is outside time and matter. He has no beginning or end. He does not undergo growth, development, or maturation. Scripture says God is eternal (Deuteronomy 33:27) and that He inhabits eternity (Isaiah 57:15). Although God is timeless, time is His creation, and history is the arena of His work. We cannot comprehend His eternality because we live in a time-driven and aging world. Man could not have written about the eternality of God apart from revelation given by Him.

We also see in Scripture where He is called the everlasting God. The title Everlasting God describes His relationship toward His creation, which unlike God Himself has a beginning, whereas Eternal God is an attribute of who God is without any relationship to creation. For example, Psalm 41:13 says, "Blessed be the LORD God of Israel from everlasting to everlasting!" and Isaiah 40:28 says, "The everlasting God, the LORD, the Creator of the ends of the earth, neither faints nor is weary." Here Everlasting God is in relationship to His creation. To help understand this we can look at Jesus' body as an example. While the Son Himself is eternal, His body had a beginning when it was formed within Mary, and His body is also everlasting. Human beings are also everlasting, having a beginning but no end. Being eternal without a beginning is not fully comprehensible to our finite minds.

9. **Read Isaiah 9:6, Matthew 1:20–23, and Luke 1:35. Who is this Child? Describe which part of Him is eternal and which part is everlasting.**

____

____

____

He Is Immense and Omnipresent

Immense has to do with size. God is vast, and He cannot be measured nor contained. We understand that He is larger than His creation. He is also omnipresent, meaning He is 100 percent present with everyone, everywhere in His creation. He is immense and omnipresent at the same time, and this is incomprehensible to our finite minds.

10. **Read Psalm 139:6–12 and Jeremiah 23:23–24. Where can you go to hide from God?**

____

____

11. **Read 1 Corinthians 3:16–17 and 6:19 and 2 Corinthians 1:22. Where is the Holy Spirit in relation to all believers?**

____

____

He Is Immutable

Immutable means unchanging or constant. God never changes, meaning He is faithful to Himself and to His covenants, prophesies, promises, and works. He remains forever the same true God who never changes from within or because of anything outside Himself.

12. **Read Malachi 3:6, Hebrews 6:17, and James 1:17. What do you learn about the unchangeable character of God?**

____

____

There are times we read in the Bible that God is sorry, relenting, regretting, repenting, or changing His mind (Genesis 6:6–7; 1 Samuel 15:11; Jonah 3:10). We may think this contradicts His immutability, but it does not. In His holiness and righteousness God abhors sin and reacts against it. His position on sin never changes. However, in His grace and mercy, God always forgives those who repent. His actions change depending on the heart of the human He is interacting with, but He Himself does not change. This, too, is not fully comprehensible.

13. **Read Jonah 3:5–10. Who relented concerning the judgment of Nineveh and why?**

____

____

____

14. **Read Jonah 4:1–2. What aspects of God's character responded to the change in the Ninevites?**

____

____

____

He Is Independent

God's independence or self-existence means that He is not dependent upon anything outside Himself. He is self-sufficient in His existence and in all His works. God has life in Himself (John 5:26) and "gives to all humans life, breath, and all things" (Acts 17:25). To Israel, He revealed Himself as "I AM" (Exodus 3:14), which means the Self-Existent One. God continues to work out His will in the world, and even though He uses various means, His independence remains intact. He does not need anyone or anything except the fellowship of the Godhead. The fact that He does not need us but wants us is incomprehensible.

He Is a Self-Existent Spirit

God is Spirit, which indicates that He is not physical and is invisible. The invisible God cannot be seen by human eyes (Exodus 33:20). Because of this, the second commandment forbids making any visible representation of God (Exodus 20:4). Since God is Spirit, He must be worshiped in spirit and in truth (John 4:24).

His spirituality is incomprehensible because the invisible God sits in Heaven as if He has shape (Ephesians 1:20). He is often described with human attributes: eyes, ears, arms, hands, etc. His invisible nature is often manifested in a physical body, such as the Angel of the Lord in the Old Testament (Psalm 34:7; Genesis 16:7). Additionally, the Son, who was always Spirit, took on a physical body when He came to Earth and will retain that body throughout eternity. It is incomprehensible how God the Father can be without shape or restricted in size and yet be on His throne in Heaven.

He Is Unified

God is unified in the Trinity as God the Father, God the Son, and God the Holy Spirit. God's unity is an expression of monotheism (one God), and He is the only living, true God (Deuteronomy 6:4; Mark 12:29; John 17:11; 21–22; 1 John 5:7). His unity is incomprehensible because the God of Scripture often manifests Himself in different ways, and sometimes He even manifests Himself differently in the same passage.

15. **Read Matthew 3:13–17. List the three ways the unified God manifests Himself.**

____

____

____

God the Father's Comprehensible Attributes

God's comprehensible attributes are relatable to us because we can, to an extent, understand, possess, and practice them. However, as finite beings, humans can only share these relatable attributes but never to the same magnitude as God. For example, God is love (1 John 4:8), God is just (Isaiah 45:21), and God is Creator (Isaiah 40:28). While humans love, have a sense of justice, and are creative, we often do so imperfectly and fall short of the standards of God. Humans are creative, but we cannot create from nothing as God has done.

Comprehensible Attributes*	Verses
He is omniscient.	Ps. 139:4; Rom. 11:33–36; 1 John 3:20
He is truth.	Deut. 32:4; Ps. 31:5; John 14:6
He is wise.	Job 9:4; 1 Tim. 1:17; Jude 1:25
He is holy.	Lev. 19:2; Isa. 6:3; 43:15; John 17:11
He is Father.	Matt. 6:6–9; Rom. 4:1; 8:15, Gal. 4:6; 1 John 3:1
He is good.	1 Chron. 16:34; Matt. 19:16–17
He is love.	Eph. 2:4; 1 John 4:8
He is Savior.	Isa. 43:11; Hos. 13:4; 1 Tim. 4:10
He has a will.	Matt. 7:21; Eph. 1:11; 1 John 2:17
He is omnipotent.	Job 42:2; Jer. 32:17; Matt. 19:26
He is sovereign.	Ps. 33:9–11; Ps. 115:3; Eph. 1:11

*Listed in no particular order and not an exhaustive list

He Is Omniscient

God is omniscient, meaning He is all-knowing; He knows everything past, present, and future (Isaiah 46:10), and He knows it all right now. His knowledge does not grow or change. God's righteous judgment is rooted in the fact that He knows our secret thoughts (Psalm 94:11) and the intentions of our heart. He knows what we are going to say even before we speak (Psalm 139:4).

This attribute of knowing is shared by mankind to a limited degree. Though God knows everything, we know only in part (1 Corinthians 13:9). We are ignorant at times, and we often misunderstand, but God's knowledge is perfect. The psalmist finds His knowledge to be a source of comfort and wonder (Psalm 139:1–5).

16. **Read Psalm 139:1–18. List how God's omniscience, immensity, and omnipresence are a source of comfort to you.**

____

____

______________________   ____________________

____

____

He Is Truth

God is honest, trustworthy, forthright, and reliable. He is faithful to Himself, to His Word, and to His promises (2 Timothy 2:13). He doesn't just possess truth; He is the source of all truth. Jesus is the complete embodiment of what truth looks and sounds like. In John 14:6, Jesus declared Himself to be the way, the truth, and the life.

Though we will never be the source of all truth, our lives can and should reflect the truth of God (Deuteronomy 32:4) as we walk in the light of God's Word (1 John 1:5–7).

He Is Wise

Wisdom is the application of knowledge. God's wisdom indicates He uses His knowledge to achieve His goals. God's works are varied, but they are done in wisdom (Psalm 104:24). This includes creation (Proverbs 3:19), the partial hardening and eventual salvation of Israel (Romans 11:25–33), and redemption through Jesus Christ (1 Corinthians 1:18–25). God has always been perfectly wise (Proverbs 8). He never had to acquire wisdom, nor does He grow in it.

His wisdom is available to mankind, though it is not naturally part of our character as it is with God. We must seek wisdom through the Word of God and prayer. Both Proverbs 9:10 and Psalm 111:10 say, "The fear of the Lord is the beginning of wisdom." Therefore, godly wisdom is available to those who love and fear Him.

17. **Read James 1:5–8. What should you do if you lack wisdom either generally or in a specific area?**

He Is Holy

The Father is described as holy (1 Samuel 6:20; John 17:11). The root idea of holiness is to be separate or set apart, and because of His inherent holiness God is distinct from everything impure or unholy. God's holiness represents Him as majestic, pure, perfect, and excellent. He alone is eternally holy. In heaven the angels and the four living creatures praise God day and night, calling out, "Holy, Holy, Holy" (Isaiah 6:3).

God's holiness is an attribute that, while not inherently part of the human race, is God's goal for believers (1 Peter 1:14–16). As we grow in the grace and knowledge of our Lord, we grow in holiness (Ephesians 4:20–24). Over the course of our lives, He also disciplines us so we can partake in His holiness (Hebrews 12:10).

18. **Read Hebrews 12:1–2. The author provides a description of a marathon. What are you doing to lay aside the weights and sins in your life in order to grow in holiness?**

____

____

____

____

He Is Father

God is called Father sixteen times in the Old Testament. This paternal name is generally used to describe His relationship with Israel. Examples include the Father who bought us (Deuteronomy 32:6), the Father who created us (Malachi 2:10), and Father to Solomon during his kingship in Chronicles (1 Chronicles 22:10; 28:6).

The New Testament emphasizes the unique and mysterious relationship of God the Father with God the Son. Jesus names God as Father 193 times in the Gospels. He says in John 10:30, "I and My Father are one." When Jesus was asked to show the disciples the Father, Jesus said, "He who has seen Me has seen the Father" (John 14:9). Jesus, as the Father's Son on Earth, is the express image of the Father in Heaven (Hebrews 1:1–3).

We see the personal nature of God as our Father over 150 times in the Gospels and nearly eighty times in Acts through Revelation. Through Jesus we have been adopted as sons and daughters and are able to cry out to God as Abba Father. Through the Father's great love that He bestowed upon us we are called the children of God. Let us be ever grateful for our Father's availability and generosity to us (1 John 3:1).

This attribute of Father is shared by men who make themselves available to their children, listening to them and loving them as God the Father listens to and loves us.

19. **Read Romans 8:32. Write down what you want your Heavenly Father to give you. Discuss and pray about it with your Discipler.**

____

____

____

He Is Good

God's attribute of good means that He is always moral, never bad, and never evil (1 John 1:5). God deals bountifully and kindly with all His creatures. Psalm 145:9 says, "The LORD is good to all," and Psalm 119:68, "You are good, and do good."

20. **Read Matthew 5:45. What is the general goodness that God gives to everyone?**

____

____

____

His good nature is reflected by mankind as we live out biblical, moral principles (Luke 6:27–36) and as we praise Him for His goodness (1 Chronicles 16:34).

21. **Read Matthew 19:16–22. Who is good in this passage?**

____

____

____

22. **What commandment is missing that the rich young ruler was not doing to reflect God's goodness? (Hint: Exodus 20:12–17.)**

____

____

____

He Is Love

As with all the attributes of God, His love is eternal, meaning it has no beginning and no end. God shows His love to the world through His providential care in creation as He gives life and breath and as He faithfully keeps His promises in the Bible. God's love poured out on undeserving sinners is called grace (Ephesians 1:5–6; 2:7–9). When He shows love to those in misery and distress, it's called compassion. His love toward un-repentant sinners restrains His judgment that will come. His long-suffering allows more time for the sinner to repent.

23. **Read John 3:16, Romans 5:8, and 1 John 4:9–10. What is the chief manifestation of God's love toward us?**

This attribute of love is shared by disciples. As we receive the love of God through Jesus Christ, we are commanded to give it away to others. God's love is primarily seen through our actions and is not dependent on feelings of love for others. We are able to love others as God does because we have the indwelling of the Holy Spirit. As we demonstrate God's love, people will see Jesus in us and be drawn to Him.

24. **Read 1 Corinthians 13. List all the ways we are to demonstrate God's love to others.**

He Is Savior

God is Savior, and even before creation it was part of who He is. In 2 Peter 3:9 we see God's heart: "The Lord is not slack concerning His promise, as some count slackness, but is longsuffering toward us, not willing that any should perish but that all should come to repentance."

25. **Read Ezekiel 33:11 and 1 Timothy 2:3–4. What is God's desire?**

____

____

____

26. **Read 1 Timothy 4:10. If God is the Savior of all men, then why aren't all men saved?**

____

____

____

God is the only savior; there is no other. Hosea 13:4 reads, "Yet I am the LORD your God ever since the land of Egypt, and you shall know no God but Me; for there is no savior besides Me."

27. **Read 2 Corinthians 5:18–20. If God is the Savior, what is our responsibility as co-laborers with Him?**

____

____

____

He Has a Will

God's will bears witness to the divine authority with which He rules over creation. He does whatever He wills, in His sovereign good pleasure, because as King over creation He rules over the affairs of human beings and nations. He works all things according to the counsel of His revealed will (Ephesians 1:11). God's sovereign will is not arbitrary; it is righteous and holy.

This attribute of will is shared by mankind as we seek to know His will and purpose to do it.

28. **Read Psalm 143:10. Write out a specific prayer in an area of need asking God to align your will to the will of God.**

____

____

____

____

He Is Omnipotent

Omnipotent means all-powerful or almighty (Revelation 11:17), and it is only used of God showing that He is ruler over everyone and everything forever (Psalm 66:7). Nothing is too hard for the Lord God Almighty (Genesis 18:14; Jeremiah 32:27; Matthew 19:26). There are many examples of His power. He preserves the universe by the power of His word (Hebrews 1:3), He prevails over His enemies (Psalm 66:3), He controls the weather (Psalm 78:26; Amos 4:7), and He raised Jesus from the dead (Ephesians 1:19–20). The gospel is the power of God to save everyone who believes (Romans 1:16), keeping and protecting believers until the end (1 Peter 1:5).

This attribute of omnipotence is minimally relatable by mankind, as we receive His power through the Holy Spirit to share the gospel (Acts 1:8), to live victoriously each day (2 Corinthians 2:14; Ephesians 3:20–21; Colossians 1:9–12), and to suffer for the gospel (2 Timothy 1:7–8).

29. **Read 1 Peter 1:3–5. Describe the confidence you feel knowing the power behind your salvation.**

____

____

____

____

____

He Is Sovereign

Omnipotence and sovereignty are closely related attributes. While omnipotence emphasizes God's unlimited capacity to rule, sovereignty refers to His authority to rule. His authority is without boundaries, controls, or limits unless they are self-imposed or He chooses to give authority to others beneath Him. His sovereignty is driven by His love and is linked to His omnipotence. There are no places or persons in the universe who can exclude Him or His sovereignty, and no power in the universe can thwart His sovereign will unless He chooses to limit or restrain Himself. For example, God can love everyone and grant free will to everyone and at the same time sovereignly allow them to make their own choices in their journey to either Heaven or Hell.

To obtain the proper perspective about God's sovereignty, the question isn't "How does a sovereign God show love?" but rather "How does a loving God act sovereignly?" It is God's love that drives His sovereignty and all His other attributes. He accomplishes His will without violating mankind's God-given free will.

This attribute of sovereignty is shared by mankind in a small way, as we exercise the free will given to us by God by making decisions regarding our lives, including the decision whether to choose or to reject Him.

30. **Read Joshua 24:15. What sovereign choice was given to the twelve tribes of Israel?**

____

____

____

____

31. **Read John 3:16–19, John 20:31, John 5:24, and 1 John 5:10. What sovereign choice are we given?**

____

____

____

____

32. **Read John 6:35–40. What sovereign choice is Jesus asking the Jews to make?**

Summary of God's Attributes

All the attributes of God, those that are His alone and those that are understood and shared by mankind, define and illuminate who He is and why He is owed all our love and devotion.

Summary and Transition to Chapter 7

We have looked carefully at God the Son, God the Holy Spirit, and God the Father. We will now look at how all three are unified as one in the Trinity.

Chapter 7:

The Trinity

This chapter will discuss the following topics:
The Unity of God in the Old Testament
The Plurality of the Godhead
Six Lines of Evidence for the Plurality of God
The Trinity or Triunity of God in the New Testament
The Difficult Doctrine of the Triunity of God
The Trinity Works Together in Attornment
The Trinity Works Together at the Cross
The Trinity Works Together in the Resurrection
The Trinity Works Together to Complete Our Redemption
The Trinity Works Together to Form the Church
Ode to Our Glorious God

Having studied God the Father, God the Son, and God the Holy Spirit, we will now focus on their unity. The Old Testament emphasizes the unity of God with hints of plurality in the Godhead, while the New Testament clearly emphasizes the work of the Triune Godhead to save mankind and fulfill the promises and prophesies of the Old Testament, particularly concerning Israel. This was accomplished through the shed blood of Jesus Christ, which ushered in the New Covenant seen in Jeremiah 31:31–34 and Matthew 26:28. In the New Testament we see the Godhead as three equal persons, working in harmony, finishing the work of judgment and redemption promised in Genesis 3:15. The New Testament calls the three persons who work together by one name, God. The Church has traditionally called this threefold manifestation the Trinity.

1. **Read Deuteronomy 6:4 and Ephesians 4:4–6. Describe the ways the word *one* is used concerning the Godhead and its unity.**

God is a unified whole. These three distinct persons are working together to accomplish our redemption in the New Testament.

The Unity of God in the Old Testament

Unity means that there is only one God and His divine nature or essence is undivided and indivisible. This is the great truth of the Old Testament (Deuteronomy 4:35, 39; 1 Kings 8:60; Isaiah 45:5). The same truth is frequently taught in the New Testament (Mark 12:29–32; 1 Corinthians 8:4–6). God is not merely one; He is the only God. There is only one infinite and perfect Being. He is unique (Exodus 15:11; 1 Kings 8:23).

Deuteronomy 6:4 reads, "Hear, O Israel: The LORD our God, the LORD is one!" In this verse God is Elohim, which is in the plural. The word *one* describes Him as multifaceted yet unified. It is the same word used to describe a husband and wife's oneness when God says that the two shall be one flesh (Genesis 2:24).

2. **Read Matthew 28:19. Why does Jesus say to baptize in the name and not names?**

The unity of God allows for the existence of personal distinctions in the one divine essence, while at the same time recognizing that the divine essence is numerically and eternally one. Many sects and cults have broken with the historical Christian faith at this point by failing to accept the doctrine of three persons but one essence.

3. **Read John 5:19, John 6:38–40, and John 17:4–5. What is the Father-Son relationship?**

____

____

____

4. **Read Hebrews 1:1–12. What else do you learn about the Father-Son relationship?**

____

____

____

God the Father and God the Son have been eternally unified in the Father-Son relationship. The New Testament emphasizes this relationship, as Jesus refers to God as Father over 190 times in the four Gospels. This eternal relationship is one of submission on the part of the Son.

The Holy Spirit is also unified with the Father and the Son. The Spirit purposes to fulfill God's will in everything He does. The Father and the Son work together through the Holy Spirit to bring many sons and daughters into the family of God.

5. **Read Matthew 10:20, John 14:26, 15:26, 16:13, and Acts 5:32. How do these verses show the Holy Spirit's unity and submission with the Father and the Son?**

____

____

____

____

The Plurality of the Godhead

In this section we will show the plurality of the Godhead, based on grammar and six evidences in Scripture for the plurality of the Godhead.

The Grammar of Plurality

God created language, and language uses grammar. Grammar is important for a proper understanding about who God is and what He wants us to comprehend in the Scriptures. It is God who chose to communicate originally in the Hebrew and Greek languages. In these original languages of the Scriptures, grammar helps to show the uniqueness of God. While all languages struggle to describe perfectly the infinite God, the original languages give us the most accurate picture.

The Hebrew word for God that is most often used in the Old Testament is Elohim. It is used of both the true God (Genesis 1:1) and the many false gods (Exodus 20:3; Deuteronomy 13:2). English translations are not always clear which God/gods are being referenced, and while we can use context clues, Hebrew grammar and context will always make it clear. The one true God is generally a Hebrew masculine plural noun followed by a singular verb in the Hebrew language.

> **Elohim in the Hebrew**
>
> Elohim + singular verb/adjective = The One True God (Gen. 1:1)
>
> Elohim + plural verbs/adjectives = false gods (Ex. 20:3)

Genesis 1:1 says, "In the beginning God [Elohim] created the heavens and the earth." Here in Genesis 1:1, the singular verb is *bara*. Therefore, since Elohim is plural but bara is singular, it is speaking of the true God.

> אֱלֹהִים – Elohim: is the plural form for God
>
> בָּרָא – Bara (created): singular verb

Exodus 20:3 says, "You shall have no other gods [elohim] before Me." The word *other*, *akharim*, is a plural adjective, showing that *elohim* here is speaking of false gods.

> אֲחֵרִים – Akhairim: plural adjective meaning other

Another grammatical example of the plurality of God is seen in Genesis 11:7: "Come, let Us go down and there confuse their language, that they may not understand one another's speech." *Us* suggests more than one person in the Godhead. The exact number comprising this plurality is not revealed in the Old Testament, though the concepts surrounding plural unity are revealed. The exact number of the plurality of God is revealed in the New Testament. The Hebrew word for God in this verse, Elohim, is a plural noun when speaking of the one true God. This opens the door to the concept of plurality and our understanding of the Trinity, which is God the Father, God the Son, and God the Holy Spirit (Matthew 28:19).

6. **Read Genesis 1:26. Describe the hints of plurality in these verses.**

____

____

____

Six Lines of Evidence for the Plurality of God

Evidence 1: Singular and Plural Nouns

This first evidence of the plural unity of God comes from the writings of Moses in Deuteronomy 6:4. Singular and plural words are important when it comes to understanding God, His nature, and His manifested plurality. Deuteronomy 6:4 reads, "Hear, O Israel: The LORD our God, the LORD is one!" When we identify and clarify the singular versus the plural nouns in this verse, it reads this way:

"Hear, O Israel: The LORD our God, the LORD is one!"

(YHWH) (Elohim) (YHWH) (Ekhad)

(singular) (plural) (singular) (compound unity)

There is another word for one and only one in the Hebrew. Genesis 22:2 reads, "Then He said, 'Take now your son, your only son Isaac." The Hebrew word for only is *yakheed*, meaning one and only, and this word is never used of God, which indicates that God is a compound unity. God is only referred to by the compound unity Ekhad . He is not one of many multiple gods. He is one unified God comprised of more than one person.

Most of the time when the plural word *Elohim* is used of God, a singular verb is used with it to indicate through the grammar that the Scriptures are speaking of the one true God. This is contrary to normal Hebrew grammar, which prefers the verb and noun to agree in both gender and number. Though the use of the plural noun with the singular verb is unconventional, it is the most common usage for Elohim, the one true God, in the Old Testament.

When it comes to false gods, it is always a plural noun, such as elohim (gods), with a plural verb. There are a few exceptions when speaking of the one true God where we see the plural Elohim with a plural verb (Genesis 20:13; 35:7; 2 Samuel 7:23; Psalm 58:11); however, their context makes clear that Scripture is speaking of the one true God.

Evidence 2: The Name Elohim Applied to Two Persons

The second line of evidence for plurality of the Godhead in the Old Testament is that the word *Elohim*, or God, is often applied to two different persons of the Godhead within the same passage. For example, Psalm 45:6–7 reads, "Your throne, O God [Elohim, the Son], is forever and ever; a scepter of righteousness is the scepter of Your kingdom. You love righteousness and hate wickedness; Therefore God [Elohim, the Father], Your God [also Elohim, the Father], has anointed You with the oil of gladness more than Your companions." In this passage both the Son and the Father are called Elohim.

7. **Read Hebrews 1:1–12. In this passage there are many pronouns and references to God the Father and God the Son. On each line write which person of the Trinity is referred to: God the Father or God the Son.**

> [1] God ___________, who at various times and in various ways spoke in time past to the fathers by the prophets,

> [2] has in these last days spoken to us by His __________ Son, whom He __________ has appointed heir of all things, through whom __________ also He __________ made the worlds [ages];

> [3] who __________ being the brightness of His __________ glory and the express image of His__________ person, and upholding all things by the word of His __________ power, when He

__________ had by Himself purged our sins, sat down at the right hand of the Majesty __________ on high,

4 having become so much better than the angels, as He __________ has by inheritance obtained a more excellent name than they.

5 For to which of the angels did He __________ ever say, "You are My Son, today I have begotten you"? And again, "I will be to Him __________ a Father, and He __________ shall be to Me a Son"?

6 But when He __________ again brings the firstborn into the world, He __________ says: "Let all the angels of God worship Him __________."

7 And of the angels He __________ says: "Who makes His angel's spirits and His [angelic] ministers a flame of fire."

8 But to the Son He __________ says: "Your throne, O God __________, is forever and ever; a scepter of righteousness is the scepter of Your __________ kingdom.

9 You __________ have loved righteousness and hated lawlessness; therefore, God __________, Your God, has anointed You __________ with the oil of gladness more than Your companions."

10 And: "You __________, Lord, in the beginning laid the foundation of the earth, and the heavens are the work of Your hands.

11 They will perish, but You __________ remain; and they will all grow old like a garment;

12 Like a cloak You __________ will fold them up, and they will be changed. But You __________ are the same, and Your years will not fail."

This first chapter of Hebrews quotes extensively from the Old Testament, and we clearly see God the Father speaking of and honoring God the Son.

Evidence 3: The Name YHWH Applied to Two Persons

The third line of evidence for the plurality of the Godhead in the Old Testament is the fact that the personal name of God, YHWH, often translated LORD in all capital letters, is applied to two different Persons in one passage.

8. **In context Genesis 18:1 tells us that the Lord (YHWH) is on earth speaking to Abraham. Read Genesis 19:24. Identify YHWH in heaven and YHWH on Earth?**

9. **Read Judges 6:11–16. Who is the "Angel of the LORD" (hint: verses 14 and 16)?**

10. **How many YHWHs (Lords) are in verse 12?**

Knowing that only YHWH the Son appears to men and women on Earth, we see clearly from these passages that YHWH is used of plural members of the Godhead, whether on Earth or in Heaven, in the same conversations.

Evidence 4: Plural Pronouns

A fourth line of evidence for the plurality of the Godhead in the Old Testament is that plural pronouns are used of God. When YHWH speaks about Himself in the plural, He uses pronouns like Us and Our (Genesis 11:6–8). Genesis 1:26 reads, "Then God said, 'Let Us make man in Our image, according to Our likeness.'" The words *Us* and *Our* are plural pronouns referring to God. God is not including angels in these terms because man was to be created not in the image of angels but in the image of God. These personal pronouns can only be a reference to God in His plurality and not to any angel.

Evidence 5: Plural Adjectives

A fifth line of evidence that shows the plurality of the Godhead from the Old Testament is that God is sometimes described using plural adjectives. Typically, a single adjective is used for a single person; therefore, a plural adjective when applied to deity speaks to the plurality of God. For example, Joshua 24:19 mentions (in English) a "holy God," yet in Hebrew the adjective *holy* is plural, which literally reads "holies Gods."

A second example is Proverbs 9:10, "The fear of the Lord is the beginning of wisdom, and the knowledge of the Holy One is understanding." In this verse the Hebrew for "Holy One" is a plural adjective, *kadosh*, meaning "Holies." It describes the Lord and literally reads, "The fear of the Lord is the beginning of wisdom, and the knowledge of the Holies is understanding." We also see this in Joshua 24:19 and Proverbs 30:3. The word *Holy* in these verses is literally "Holies."

These plural adjectives are hidden nuggets that illuminate God's plurality within the Godhead.

Evidence 6: The Angel of the Lord

The sixth line of evidence showing the plurality of the Godhead in the Old Testament is the teachings concerning the Angel of the Lord, or literally the Angel of YHWH. In Genesis 16:7–14, in one part of the passage He is called the Angel of YHWH (LORD), and in another part of the same passage He is called YHWH (LORD), without the word *Angel*. It is clear that the Angel of YHWH is not a common, ordinary, created angel but a unique being or messenger, who is a visible manifestation of God the Son Himself. The context always makes this evident.

11. **Read Genesis 22:9–16. Which verses describe the Angel of the LORD as YHWH and why?**

____

____

____

Bridge

We now move from evidence of God's unity and hints of plurality in the Old Testament to the specifics about the trinity or triunity of God in the New Testament.

The Trinity or Triunity of God in the New Testament

The doctrine of the Trinity, or Triunity, is a great mystery, and it may even appear to some as an intellectual puzzle or a contradiction. This Christian doctrine, mysterious as it may seem, is not from speculation but of revelation. God revealed much about this doctrine in His Word.

Though the word *Trinity* is not in the Bible, it is unquestionably a biblical truth. The Old and New Testaments together present the one God who manifests Himself in three persons. The emphasis in the Old Testament is upon divine unity with evidences of plurality. The New Testament emphasizes plurality, focusing on the individual persons of the Trinity, primarily for their separate responsibilities regarding our redemption.

The New Testament gives us the exact number of persons in the Godhead, three, and it is called the Trinity. The Greek word *trias* was used very early in the church and seems to have been first used by Theophilus of Antioch in AD 181. The Latin word *trinitas* was used by Tertullian in AD 220. Both words basically mean three without any reference to three being unified as one. Over time in Christian theology, through the study of God's Word, the term *trinity* has come to mean that there are three eternal distinctions in the one divine essence, known respectively as Father, Son, and Holy Spirit. One unified God is manifested as three unique persons. When we combine the words *Trinity* (which means threefold) with *unity*, we get the clearer word *Triunity*, which is a more precise description of the Godhead.

Trinity + Unity = Triunity

The Triunity is expressed clearly in Matthew 28:19: "Go therefore and make disciples of all the nations, baptizing them in the name of the

Father and of the Son and of the Holy Spirit." The phrase "the name" is singular and not plural, indicating that the three persons are unified as the one true God. The doctrine of Triunity must be distinguished from both Tritheism and Sabellianism to further clarify the biblical view of the Triunity.

Tritheism denies the essential oneness of God and holds to three distinct gods. The only unity that it recognizes is the unity of purpose and endeavor. However, the God of the Bible is a unity of essence and nature as well as of purpose and endeavor.

Sabellianism teaches that God is one person who reveals Himself variously over time as the Father in the Old Testament, the Son in the New Testament, and the Holy Spirit today. According to Sabellianism, God is one person with three manifestations. This is different from the biblical teaching that God is three persons sharing one divine nature, all at the same time, from eternity past into eternity future.

"Burden is laid upon the student of the Bible to recognize that, regardless of how difficult the teachings of the Godhead are, we are appointed to discover and defend the truth that the Bible is monotheistic to the last degree, contending, as it does, that there is one God and only one. Yet just as certainly as it asserts that there is only one God, it asserts throughout that God subsists in three definite and identified persons" (Lewis Sperry Chafer).

The Difficult Doctrine of the Triunity of God

The doctrine of Triunity is foundational to the Christian faith, yet it also presents four difficult questions to our finite minds:

1. How can God be both one and three?
2. When Jesus prayed to God, was He praying to Himself?
3. Is the Trinity, or Triunity, a contradiction in itself?
4. Why does Jesus say the Father is greater than I?

While we cannot fully understand everything about the Triunity of God, it is possible to answer these four questions and gain a solid grasp on what it means for God to be three persons in one essence.

Question # 1: How can God be both one and three?

The doctrine of the Triunity of God expresses three crucial truths that we have already established about each member of the Godhead:

1. The Father, the Son, and the Holy Spirit are distinct persons.
2. Each person is fully God.
3. There is only one God.

The first truth states that the Bible teaches us that the Father, Son, and Holy Spirit are distinct persons.

Read Matthew 3:13–17.

At the baptism of Jesus, we see each member of the Triunity uniquely participating in the baptism, all at the same time. Jesus came up out of the water, the Spirit descended upon Jesus, and the Father spoke from heaven. They are three distinct persons who are all the one true God.

There is a clear hierarchy within the Triunity in which the Father is the head, Jesus submits to the Father, and the Spirit submits to both the Father and the Son.

12. **Read John 5:30 and John 6:38. How is Jesus showing submission?**

____

____

13. **Read John 14:26 and John 15:26, and describe the Triunity found in these verses.**

____

____

Submission does not mean inferior. None of them are inferior to the other. Instead, they are all equal and identical in power, love, mercy, justice, holiness, knowledge, and all other qualities and attributes of God.

14. **Read John 1 verses 1, 14, and 18. How are God and Jesus both the same and different from one another?**

____

____

15. **Read Romans 15:30 and 2 Corinthians 13:14. How do these verses speak of three distinct persons?**

____

____

____

____

The second truth is each person in the Triunity is fully God.

Father as God: "Grace to you and peace from God our Father and the Lord Jesus Christ." (Philippians 1:2)

Jesus as God: "Looking for the blessed hope and glorious appearing of our great God and Savior Jesus Christ." (Titus 2:13)

Holy Spirit as God: "But Peter said, 'Ananias, why has Satan filled your heart to lie to the Holy Spirit and keep back part of the price of the land for yourself? While it remained, was it not your own? And after it was sold, was it not in your own control? Why have you conceived this thing in your heart? You have not lied to men but to God.'" (Acts 5:3–4)

If God is three persons yet one God, does this mean that each person is "one third" of God? No. The doctrine of the Triunity does not divide God into three parts. We should not think of God as a "pie" cut into three pieces with each piece representing a person. This would make each person less than fully God and thus not God at all. The Bible is clear that all three persons are each 100 percent God. Colossians 2:9 says of Christ, "For in Him dwells all the fullness of the Godhead bodily." Each member of the Triunity is fully God, not one third of God.

The third truth is there is only one God.

If each person of the Triunity is distinct and yet fully God, then can we conclude that there is more than one God? Obviously, we cannot, for Scripture is clear that there is only one God. Deuteronomy 6:4 says, "Hear, O Israel: The LORD our God, the LORD is one!"

Isaiah 45:21–22 reads, "And there is no other God besides Me, a just God and a Savior; there is none besides Me. Look to Me, and be saved, all you ends of the earth! For I am God, and there is no other."

16. **Read Acts 2:32–33. Describe the Triunity according to these verses.**

____

____

17. **Read Galatians 4:6. How does Paul describe the Triunity?**

____

____

18. **Read Ephesians 2:14–18. Describe the Triunity and the role of each member of the Godhead according to these verses.**

____

____

19. **Read Ephesians 3:14–19. Describe the Triunity in these verses and the function of each person.**

____

____

20. **Read 1 Peter 1:2. Describe the Triunity in this verse.**

____

____

21. **Read 1 John 5:7. This is the most definitive verse in the Bible on the Triunity of God. Describe the Triunity in this verse.**

____

____

Scan here for a detailed defense of 1John 5:7-8 which is known as the "Johanna Comma"

Question # 2: When Jesus prayed to God, was He praying to Himself?

The Gospels record instances where Jesus prayed to God the Father. Does that mean He was praying to Himself? No. While Jesus and the Father are both God, they are different persons. Jesus prayed to God the Father without praying to Himself. In fact, the continuing dialogue between the Father and the Son furnishes the best evidence that they are distinct persons (Matthew 3:17, 17:5; John 11:41-42, 17:1-26)

Question # 3: Is the Trinity, or Triunity, a contradiction in itself?

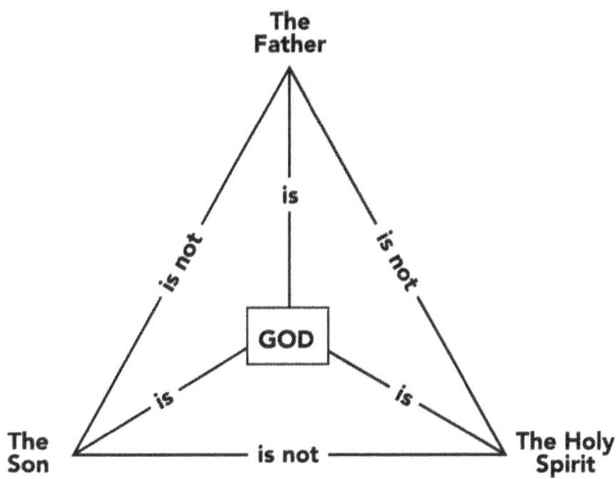

Is it a contradiction to say that the Triunity is one God in three Persons? No. A contradiction occurs only when something is A and not A at the same time. For example, a table cannot be a table and not a table at the same time. It would be a contradiction to say God is three essences in one essence or to say God is three persons in one person. However, it is not a contradiction to claim that God is three persons in one essence or three distinct personalities in one essence. God is one in essence, but three in persons. Essence and persons are distinct.

Essence is God's core nature, which is eternal and never changes; it includes his attributes such as light, love, and holiness.

Person refers to the uniqueness of the three individuals within the Godhead: the Father, the Son, and the Holy Spirit. For example, only the Father has all authority (Ephesians 4:6; 1 Corinthains 15:24), only the Son took on humanity (John 1:1, 14, and 18), and only the Holy Spirit infills the believer (John 14:17). Each person of the Triunity is completely God yet inextricably united with the other two persons.

Question #4: Why does Jesus say the Father is greater than I?

22. **Read John 14:28 and John 20:17. Notice and record how Jesus describes His relationship to the Father.**

____

____

All three members of the Godhead are equal, yet they each had different responsibilities regarding the salvation mission. When the Father sent the Son to Earth, Jesus willingly humbled Himself to become a man. He did not lose His divinity; rather, He added on humanity. As the God-man, Jesus temporarily limited His divine rights and submitted Himself to the leadership, authority, and will of the Father in order to accomplish God's mission to save mankind. Philippians 2:5–8 describes Jesus' self-imposed limitations to include the following tasks: living in a sinful broken world instead of in the perfection and praises of heaven, veiling His glory in a human body to become the servant of all, humbling Himself in obedience to the Father, and dying on a cross for all mankind. These verses demonstrate why Jesus declared that the Father was greater than Himself and the Father was His God, all while He was the divine human sacrifice as the Lamb of God.

Bridge

The Word of God clearly teaches that God is one and manifests Himself in three persons. Next, we will see why the Triunity of God makes perfect sense and how each member participates in their work on Earth.

The Triunity Works Together in Atonement

We have a better understanding of the Triunity when we realize that God the Father and God the Son agreed that the Son was to leave heaven and come down to Earth as the God-man in order to redeem us. After Jesus' work on Earth was finished and He went back to heaven, they (Father and Son) sent God the Holy Spirit to live and work in every believer and to convict everyone else of their sin of unbelief. The Triunity of God works together perfectly to offer atonement to all mankind.

The Triunity Works Together at the Cross

In Matthew 27:46 we hear God the Son fulfilling Psalm 22:1 by crying out on the cross, "My God [speaking to the Father], My God [speaking to the Holy Spirit], why have You forsaken Me?" The Son of God is bearing the punishment for our sins, and we see Him in great agony over being forsaken by God. This lasted three hours until He said, "It is finished" (John 19:30), and "Father, 'into Your hands I commit My spirit'" (Luke 23:46). At the cross we see the Triunity of God working out our atonement.

On the cross He was truly the loneliest Man who ever hung between Heaven and Earth.

As the saying goes, "When we approach the cross, we should take off our shoes, for we are standing on holy ground." (Anonymous)

Our finite minds cannot comprehend all that happened on the cross. The only person who understood the depth and magnitude and accepted it is God the Father. We understand only enough to believe, be awed, and be grateful for the work of Jesus on the cross.

The Triunity Works Together in the Resurrection

23. **For each verse below, answer the question "Who raised Jesus from the dead?"**

Galatians 1:1

John 2:19–22

1 Peter 3:18

Acts 2:24

Romans 8:11 demonstrates the Triunity of God in the resurrection: "But if the Spirit of Him [the Father] who raised Jesus from the dead dwells in you, He [the Father] who raised Christ from the dead will also give life to your mortal bodies through His [the Father's] Spirit who dwells in you."

The Triunity Works to Complete Our Redemption

The Triunity of God works together perfectly to offer atonement to all mankind. In order to redeem us, the Father sent the Son to leave heaven and come down to Earth. After Jesus' work on Earth was finished, He returned to heaven. The Father and the Son sent God the Holy Spirit to live and work in every believer and to convict the world of the sin of unbelief (John 16:8–9).

After we experience saving grace, the Triunity works to complete the journey of our salvation all the way to Heaven. Second Corinthians 1:9–10 speaks of our past, present, and future deliverance: "We had the sentence of death in ourselves, that we should not trust in ourselves but in God who raises the dead, who delivered us from so great a death, and does deliver us; in whom we trust that He will still deliver us."

24. **The verses below show the Triunity working together for our redemption. Read and record and each person of the Triunity you see and what verse they are in.**

Romans 5:1–5

Ephesians 1:3–14

---

2 Corinthians 1:19–22

Hebrews 9:13–15

Jude 24 reads, "Now to Him [God] who is able to keep you from stumbling, and to present you faultless before the presence of His glory with exceeding joy." The Triune God not only provided redemption but provided the means to complete our journey that ends before His presence with exceeding joy in heaven.

The Triunity Works to Form the Church

While on Earth Jesus told His followers that He would build His church (Matthew 16:18–21). The church would be called His body, or the Body of Christ, and Jesus would be the head of His Body (Colossians 1:18). After His death, resurrection, and ascension, He was seated at the right hand of the Father in heaven (Acts 2:33). How could He build His Church if He was no longer on Earth? The Father and Jesus sent the Helper, the Holy Spirit, to do the work (John 14:16–18; 16:7). The Holy Spirit convicts and draws unbelievers to God (John 16:8–11). At the moment of salvation, the Holy Spirit baptizes each one into the Body of Christ (1 Corinthians 12:13). This is separate from water baptism, which occurs as an act of obedience and is a testimony to the Church of one's declaration of faith in Jesus. After death, believers are no longer part of the physical church on Earth, but they continue to be a part of the Body of Christ in heaven. According to Ephesians 1:10, at the end of the church age, all of His Body will be gathered together in heaven. The Triunity is working together to form the Church.

25. **Read 1 Corinthians 12:3–6. What is the Triunity's involvement in church ministries and activities?**

____

____

____

____

26. **Read Ephesians 2:14–18. What are the activities of the Triunity in these verses on behalf of the Church?**

____

____

____

____

27. **What activity of ours is made possible by verse 18?**

____

____

____

Progressively, we have seen in the Old Testament the unity and plurality of God, then in the New Testament, that the plurality of God is threefold and how the Triunity works for our redemption, the formation of the church, and in our personal lives. These truths should result in glorious praise toward our Triune God.

Ode to Our Glorious God

You are God.
You are El Shaddai, Almighty God!
You are El Olam, the Everlasting One!
You are YHWH, the self-existent One.
You are Elohim, the God of creation and nature.
You are everywhere, fully present because You are Spirit, yet
You are totally independent of Your creation.
You are one God in essence, three in persons: the Triunity.

You are Adonai, Lord and Master of all.
You are all-knowing, the sum of all wisdom.
You are the source of truth and morality.
Your will is manifested in loving sovereignty.
You are holiness and love and justice at the same time and without contradiction.
You never change, yet Your actions change depending on our response to You.

Your relationship to man is as YHWH Elohim, the Lord God.
You are Adonai, YHWH, covenant keeper.
You are YHWH Yireh, for You see and provide the needed sacrifice for mankind.
You are YHWH Tzidkeinu, righteous and giver of righteousness to all who believe.
You are YHWH Mqaddis, for You set us apart for Your use, pleasure, and glory.

You are YHWH Tzvaot, the head of the armies of heaven.
You are YHWH Makeh, the one who smites Your enemies.
You are YHWH Nisi, the banner we rally under for protection.

You are YHWH Shalom, our peace!
You are YHWH Ro'i, our Good Shepherd.
You are YHWH Rapha, our healer.
You are YHWH Shamah, always with us! You never leave!
You are El Ro'i, the God of sight and vision, who never closes His eyes to us.

You are Theos, under the New Covenant, the true God.
You are Kurios, Lord, possessor, and ruler.
You are Despoteis, master owner.
You are Logos, the Word made flesh.
You are Jesus, the ultimate communication of God.
You are Hupsistos, the Highest. No one is above or over You.
You are Pantokrator, the Almighty.
You are to us Father, Son, and Holy Spirit. We are eternally grateful to You.

Summary and Transition to Chapter 8

Heaven's best, Jesus Christ the Son of God, came down to Earth and completed everything necessary for mankind's salvation. He ascended back to Heaven and is sitting at the right of the Father. He then sent forth His Holy Spirit to continue the work of saving mankind through each person's faith in Christ Crucified. The invisible Spirit's visible Ambassadors for spreading the good news of God's salvation were the Twelve Apostles/ Prophets of Acts chapter 1. The Twelve and Christ Crucified as the chief cornerstone comprise the foundation of the Church. The Church, as a body, is being built upon this completed foundation. We will now describe the foundation upon which the Church is being built. In book 2 of Rooted and Grounded, we will thoroughly examine the structure and functions of the Church that is being built upon this completed foundation.

Chapter 8:

The Church and Foundation

This chapter will discuss the following topics:
Foundation Gifts
Church-Building Gifts
Building on the Foundation

James 1:17 tells us, "Every good gift and every perfect gift is from above, and comes down from the Father of lights, with whom there is no variation or shadow of turning."

The Church's Foundation and building gifts are from the Son Himself, who is the head of the Church. The foundation gifts (apostles and prophets) and the building gifts (evangelists and pastors/teachers) are men. Ephesians 4:11–12 says, "He Himself [Jesus] gave some [men] to be apostles, some prophets, some evangelists, and some pastors and teachers, for the equipping of the saints for the work of ministry, for the edifying of the [Body] of Christ." In the Greek text apostles, prophets, evangelists, and pastors/teachers are always masculine. The gifts of the Holy Spirit are listed in Romans 12 and 1 Corinthians 12, and they are given to the local church and will be discussed in book 2.

Foundation Gifts

Titles	Descriptions	Verses
Apostles	The foundation gift of apostle was given by Jesus to establish the original, fundamental teachings of the church and to build upon the completed foundation of Jesus Christ, who is the Chief Cornerstone.	Luke 6:12–16; John 15:16; 1 Cor. 12:28; 9:1–2; 2 Cor.12:12; Eph. 2:20; 4:11
Prophets	The New Testament gift of prophet was given to men who received revelation from God to establish and maintain the doctrinal purity of the foundation of the church until the completion of the New Testament.	Eph. 2:20; 4:11

Apostles

Apostle, Greek, apostolos (masculine noun): A delegate, messenger, one sent forth with orders, applied to certain disciples of Jesus Christ.

All apostles are chosen by Jesus, and He prayed all night before choosing twelve to be apostles. First called "the Twelve Apostles" in Matthew 10:2, He then "sent them out" (using the verb form of apostle, which is apostello). When they returned, as we see in Mark 6:30, "the apostles gathered to Jesus and told Him all things, both what they had done and what they had taught." This would be a precursor of what the twelve would do as they laid the foundation for the Church after Christ's ascension. The miracles they performed certified their teaching. Following Peter's foundational preaching, we read that many signs and wonders were publicly done by all the Apostles (Acts 2:43).

Sometime after Jesus titled the twelve as Apostles in Matthew 10, He asked them two very important questions.

1. **Read Matthew 16:13–18. What two questions did Jesus ask, and what were the answers?**

____

____

____

The Father in Heaven made sure Peter had received the correct answer (v. 17). We have the first mention of the word *church* by Jesus (v. 18), where He declared that it was His church and He would build it.

2. **What is the foundation upon which Jesus will build His church?**

____

____

____

Peter is the key Apostle in the building of the universal Church on the finished foundation. He declared that the foundation was Christ, the Son of the living God, even though at this point (Matthew 16) Jesus had not yet died for the sins of the world. After His ascension, the formation of the Church, and the initial building of it, Paul would add a phrase to Peter's remarks to describe the completed foundation of the church.

3. **Read 1 Corinthians 2:1–5 and 3:11. What additional phrase is used to describe the completed foundation?**

____

____

4. **What action on the part of men and women is required to begin building on the foundation (v. 5)?**

____

____

According to 1 Peter 2:5 every person who believes in the foundational truth of Christ Crucified is then added as a living stone to the superstructure of the Church. The Church will continue to be built, even today, until the full number of the Gentiles is complete (Romans 11:25).

Two Tiers of Apostles

First-Tier Apostles

In Luke 6:12–16, Jesus went away, prayed all night, and then chose twelve apostles from a larger group of disciples. One of those disciples was Judas, who later betrayed Jesus and then killed himself. After the ascension of Jesus, we see the choosing of Matthias to replace Judas (Acts 1–2).

5. **Read Acts 1:15–20. How do we know that Judas needed to be replaced?**

____

____

____

6. **Read Acts 1:21–23. What qualifies a man to replace Judas?**

____

____

____

7. **Read Acts 1:24–26. Who chose Matthias?**

____

____

____

Matthias is the twelfth apostle, confirmed in Acts 2:14, whether the author of Acts refers to "Peter, standing up with the eleven." Matthias is the twelfth apostle because Peter plus eleven equals twelve. We also see in Acts 6:2, "Then the twelve," confirming Matthias as the 12th apostle. These are the first-tier apostles, and they were not replaced when they died.

There were never more than twelve first-tier apostles, even after the ascension of Jesus. We see the twelve in Acts 6:2, but after the book of Acts, the first-tier apostles are only found in two places, 1 Corinthians 15:5 and Revelation 21:14. These twelve apostles are the twelve names written on the twelve foundations of the New Jerusalem in Revelation 21:14, and are referred to as "the twelve apostles of the Lamb." There were only twelve first-tier Apostles, and they were also Prophets.

The Twelve Apostles

The first-tier apostles were always called "the twelve" even when there were only eleven after Judas' departure and death. In John 20:24 Judas was gone and was not yet replaced by Matthias, but the Holy Spirit officially refers to the apostles as the twelve: "Now Thomas, called the twin, one of the twelve, was not with them when Jesus came" (also see Matthew 28:16; Luke 24:33; Acts 1:26; 2:14). We also see the official title of the twelve in 1 Corinthians 15:4–5: "He was buried, and that He rose again the third day according to the Scriptures, and that He was seen by Cephas, then by the twelve." These sightings were all before Matthias was chosen to replace Judas, yet Paul collectively refers to the first-tier apostles by their title, the Twelve.

We see the Old Testament precedence for referring to a group with varying numbers as "the Twelve." The tribes of Israel were designated the twelve tribes, even after Joseph's inheritance was divided up between his two sons Ephraim and Manasseh, which made for thirteen tribes. But they were never called the thirteen tribes, only the twelve tribes of Israel. One could argue that Levi was not a land inheritor and therefore not a part of the twelve. However, in Revelation 7 Levi is listed as one of the twelve, while Dan is excluded. Dan reappears in the listing of the twelve in the Kingdom Age in Ezekiel 48. Whenever the tribes are listed after Jacob adopted the sons of Joseph, only twelve of thirteen are listed. One of the thirteen is always missing.

Interestingly, various biblical lists of the tribes differ in both the number and names included. For instance, the Song of Deborah lists only ten tribes, omitting Judah, Simeon, and Levi. The Blessing of Moses mentions eleven tribes, excluding Simeon. Some lists maintain twelve by omitting Levi and separating Ephraim and Manasseh.

In the new heavens and new earth, in the New Jerusalem, we find both sets of twelve, the Twelve Tribes of Israel and the Twelve Apostles. Revelation 21:12 says, "Also she had a great and high wall with twelve gates, and twelve angels at the gates, and names written on them, which are the names of the **twelve tribes** of the children of Israel." And Revelation 21:14 reads, "Now the wall of the city had twelve foundations, and on them were the names of the **twelve apostles** of the Lamb."

Though actual numbers may vary, they are known as the Twelve Tribes of Israel. Though the first-tier apostles became eleven in number for a while, they also are titled the Twelve or the Twelve Apostles.

Second-Tier Apostles

The second-tier apostles were not a part of Christ's ministry before His cross; however, they saw Jesus after His resurrection. Paul fulfilled this requirement because He saw the risen Christ (see Acts 9:27; 26:12–18; 1 Corinthians 15:8, and Galatians 1:11–12). Paul calls himself an apostle in the first verse of many of his letters, including Romans, 1 and 2 Corinthians, Galatians, Ephesians, Colossians, 1 and 2 Timothy, and Titus.

8. **Read Acts 9:27 and 1 Corinthians 9:1. What defense does Paul give for his apostleship?**

____

____

____

By the time Paul wrote Ephesians, the building foundation of the Church by the first-tier apostles and prophets was already completed. Ephesians 2:19–20 says, "Now, therefore, you are no longer strangers and foreigners, but fellow citizens with the saints and members of the household of God, having been built on the [completed] foundation of the apostles and prophets, Jesus Christ Himself being the chief cornerstone." Therefore, Paul, who built upon the completed foundation, could not have been a first-tier Apostle but rather a second-tier Apostle. In 1 Corinthians 3:9–12 the Apostle Paul talks about how he laid down or affirmed the teaching of the completed foundation in the local church: "For we are God's fellow workers; you are God's field; you are God's building [built on the foundation]. According to the grace of God, which was given to me [Paul], as a wise master builder, I [Paul] have laid [down] the foundation, and another builds on it [above the finished foundation]. But let each one take heed how he builds on it [the finished foundation].

For no other [finished] foundation can anyone lay than that which is [already] laid, which is Jesus Christ [the cornerstone of Ephesians 2:20]."

In other words, Paul took these foundational teachings of the Apostles and Prophets with Jesus Christ being the Chief Cornerstone and gave them to the churches. Paul was not the only second-tier apostle, although he was the most prominent.

9. **Read 1 Corinthians 15:7–9, Galatians 1:19, Acts 14:14, and 1 Thessalonians 1:1 and 2:6. Who else was named as an apostle of this second-tier group?**

____

____

____

Signs and Wonders by Both Tiers of Apostles

Another qualification for first- and second-tier apostles included signs and wonders being performed through them (Acts 5:12; 15:12). The power of multiple signs and wonders was evidence of apostolic authority. These signs and wonders were numerous and very public. These signs and wonders affirmed and gave authority to their teaching throughout the New Testament and became known as the Apostles' Doctrine (Acts 2:41–43).

Prophets

> **Prophet, Greek:** *prophetes (masculine noun)*: One who speaks forth God's Word, generally an exhortation from inspired Scripture and at times foretelling the future. New Testament prophets were to authoritatively speak the Word of God to the church in the years before the New Testament was complete.

Generally, prophets exhorted the people to repent and turn from their wicked ways and worship the one true God with holy living. Some would also foretell the future. Sometimes, the spoken words of Old Testament and New Testament prophets became the inspired Word of God. The phrase "the word of the Lord," which was spoken by the prophets, is found 248 times in the Old Testament and fourteen times in the New Testament, mostly in the book of Acts where there was very little of the written New Testament available to believers. New Testament prophets under the New Covenant expounded this truth also known as the Apostles' Doctrine (Acts 2:42; 15:32).

10. **Read Ephesians 2:20. Who were the Apostles and Prophets in the already laid down foundation?**

____

____

Jesus refers to His twelve empowered disciples as apostles for the first time in Matthew 10:1–4, where He also names them. He also refers to these first-tier apostles as prophets in Matthew 10:40–41: "He who receives you receives Me, and he who receives Me receives Him who sent Me. He who receives a prophet in the name of a prophet shall receive a prophet's reward." There are no other men named as prophets between Matthew 10 and when the foundation of Jesus Christ was laid by the Apostles, especially by the teachings of Peter, in the early chapters of Acts.

Today, evangelists, pastor-teachers, missionaries, and those doing the work of evangelists are laying down on this completed foundation established by the Apostles and Prophets throughout the world.

11. **Read 1 Peter 2:4–6. What picture is given of the believers in relation to the cornerstone, Jesus Christ?**

____

____

____

The foundation gift of prophet was given to certain men in the early church (Ephesians 4:11). They heard from the Lord and proclaimed His message to the first-century believers. Each message that was considered inspired Scripture was added to the canon of Scripture until it was complete. Together with the apostles, the prophets formed and maintained the integrity of the Church's completed foundation, with Christ being the Chief Cornerstone (Ephesians 2:20). Like the foundation gift of apostle, the foundation gift of prophet was also temporary, ending at the close of the first century when the New Testament canon was complete.

The twelve first-tier apostles and prophets are the completed foundation of the Church, with Christ as the Chief Cornerstone (Ephesians 2:20). This means that Paul, James, Barnabas, Silvanus, and Timothy became apostles after the foundation was complete. As the apostle to the Gentiles, Paul did not build upon a new foundation but on the completed foundation of Christ and the first-tier apostles and prophets.

"The foundation of the apostles and prophets refers to the divine revelation that they taught, which in its written form is the New Testament. The meaning is not that the apostles and prophets were themselves the foundation—though in a certain sense they were—but that they laid the foundation. Paul spoke of himself as "a wise master builder" who "laid the foundation" and went on to say, "For no other foundation can anyone lay than that which is laid, which is Jesus Christ" (1 Corinthians 3:10–11). These are New Testament prophets, as indicated by the facts that they are listed after the apostles and are part of the building of the Church of Jesus Christ (Ephesians 3:5; 4:11). Their unique function was to authoritatively speak the Word of God to the Church in the years before the New Testament canon was complete. The fact that they are identified with the foundation reveals that they were limited to that formative period. As Ephesians 4:11 shows, they completed their work and gave way to "evangelists, and . . . pastors and teachers" (John McArthur, *Ephesians: The MacArthur New Testament Commentary*).

Prophet messages were generally one of two types, **predictive or foretelling,** which were revelations from God about the future (Acts 11:28; 21:10–14). Other examples include 1 Corinthians 15:51–52, 1 Thessalonians 4:13–18 and 5:1–11, 2 Thessalonians 1 and 2, 1 Timothy 4:1–3, and the entire book of Revelation. However, the primary message of all prophets, whether in the New or Old Testament, was **forthtelling**, which was exhorting the people to holy living through corrective teaching and encouragement. The early Christians did not have the complete Bible, and some early Christians did not have access to any of the books of the New Testament, so the prophets proclaimed God's message to the people who would not have had access to it otherwise. An example of forthtelling is seen as the prophets proclaiming God's unchanging gospel and His moral standards. We can affirm this principle from the fact that we have nine of the Ten Commandments included in the laws of Christ for the Church Age (Romans 13:8–10).

The foundational prophets proclaimed these truths to the Church, and they countered the many false teachers and false prophets who went out and proclaimed their false messages to the churches (2 Corinthians 11:13–14; 2 Peter 2:1; 1 John 2:18; 4:1).

12. **Read Luke 11:49, Ephesians 2:19–22, 3:1–5, and 4:11–13. What titles are linked together?**

13. **Read 2 Peter 1:16–21. How are the prophets described? Who inspired them to speak and write the books of the Bible?**

All Apostles Are Prophets

> Woe to you [lawyers]! For you build the tombs of the prophets, and your fathers killed them. In fact, you bear witness that you approve the deeds of your fathers; for they indeed killed them, and you build their tombs. Therefore the wisdom of God also said, 'I will send them prophets and apostles, and some of them they will kill and persecute,' that the blood of all the prophets which was shed from the foundation of the world may be required of this generation. (Luke 11:47–50)

Church tradition tells us that all the apostles were murdered as prophets, except the apostle John. They continued to preach the foundational messages of Peter and did not deviate, nor did they recant their faith. The apostle/prophet Paul did the same and suffered the same violent death.

The twelve first-tier apostles and prophets are the completed foundation of the church, with Christ as the Chief Cornerstone (Eph. 2:20). This means that Paul, James, Barnabas, Silvanus, and Timothy, became apostles after the foundation was complete. As the apostle to the Gentiles Paul did not build upon a new foundation but on the completed foundation of Christ and the first-tier apostles and prophets.

All Apostles are prophets, and their messages hold true to the core Apostolic Doctrine.

Were the second-tier apostles, like Paul, also prophets? New Testament prophets maintained the purity and consistency of the Apostles' Doctrine, until the completion of the inspired Scriptures at the end of the first century. We read in the completed New Testament that many false teachers and prophets followed after the apostles and prophets with their false teachings in newly planted churches (Galatians 1:6–9; 1 Timothy 1:3; 2 Timothy 2:17; 2 Peter 2:1). It was essential that the apostles were also prophets proclaiming the truths of the Apostolic Doctrine under the New Testament, or New Covenant. Not only were all first-century apostles also prophets, but they were also church builders, evangelists, and pastor-teachers, as seen by their fruit and their writings. Simply put, evangelists are recognized because of the many souls that are saved when they preach the gospel. We see the pastor/shepherd/teaching role of the apostles throughout their letters, to care for God's church. They feed the flock of God by teaching them His Word, the Apostles' Doctrine.

All apostles are prophets, but not all who are New Testament prophets are apostles.

14. **Read Acts 11:27–28, 15:25–27 along with verse 32. Who are the prophets mentioned here?**

____

____

____

Women Have Not Been Appointed Prophets by God in the Church Age

The word *prophetess* is found only twice in the New Testament. The first usage is in Luke 2:36, where we read in the first part of the verse, "Now there was one, Anna, a prophetess, the daughter of Phanuel, of the tribe of Asher." She was an Old Testament prophetess, operating under the Law of Moses; therefore, Anna was not a prophetess for the Church Age. Remember that the Church Age, under the New Covenant, did not start until Pentecost in Acts 2. The other usage of *prophetess* is by Jesus in Revelation 2:20, where He refers to a false prophetess: "Nevertheless, I have a few things against you, because you allow that woman Jezebel, who calls herself a prophetess, to teach and seduce My servants to commit sexual immorality and eat things sacrificed to idols." Nowhere in the Church Age is a woman called by God to be a prophetess. However, we see women with the gift of prophecy under the New Covenant in the Church Age. For example, in Acts 21:9 we read of Philip's daughters prophesying.

> We do not have instructions for the beginning of the Church Age for anyone desiring the office of apostle or prophet.
>
> We can conclude that there are no apostles or prophets today.

Foundation Gift of Prophet Versus the Gift of Prophecy

In 1 Corinthians 11:5 we read of women prophesying. Many assume that if a man or woman prophesies, they are a prophet or prophetess. Remember, the gift of prophet is a person (Ephesians 4:11). The gift of prophecy is a gift of the Holy Spirit given to anyone He chooses, as He wills (1 Corinthians 12:11–12), and it may or may not be permanent. The gift of prophecy has limitations on its scope of application, for 1 Corinthians 14:3 says, "But he who prophesies speaks edification and exhortation and comfort to men." Exercising the gift of prophecy does not make a prophet. Jesus gives men as prophets, and the Holy Spirit gives the gift of prophecy to whomever He chooses in the Church, male or female.

Foundation Gifts of Apostles and Prophets Do Not Exist Today

There are criteria for any man who claims to have the Gift of Apostle.

15. **Read 1 Corinthians 9:1. Here, Paul is defending his Apostleship. What is an important criterion in this verse for being an Apostle?**

____

____

____

16. **Read 2 Corinthians 12:12. What is another criterion for being an Apostle?**

____

____

____

Signs and wonders were accomplished by Jesus and the Apostles in the New Testament: by Christ in Acts 2:22; by the twelve Apostles in Acts 2:43, 4:29–30, and 5:12; by Peter in Acts 5:15; and by Paul in Acts 14:3, 19:11–12 and Romans 15:18–19. The many signs and wonders spoken as verification of the Messiahship of Jesus and the apostleship of the Twelve and of Paul do not happen today. Although many in the Church Age claim to perform signs and wonders, they are not prolific nor are they performed in the public arena for all to see and verify. Matthew 24:24 warns that before His second coming, false christs and false prophets will perform many signs and wonders.

The offices of apostles and prophets ended when the foundation of the Church was completed early in the first century. We do not have instructions for affirming anyone desiring the foundation gift of apostle or prophet, like we have for pastor-teachers in 1 Timothy 3 and Titus 2. If there is apostolic and prophetic succession after the foundation of the Church was built, instructions on affirming them would have been essential, considering that false prophets, false brethren, false apostles, and false teachers are often mentioned and warned about by Paul, Peter, John, and Jude in their letters.

17. **Read 2 Corinthians 11:13–15, 2 Peter 2:1, and Jude:4. How are the men in these verses identified, and what do they teach?**

____

____

____

Those who wrongfully teach the restoration of the office of prophet or apostle also teach that the men who claim to be apostles and prophets should never be spoken against nor questioned, because the person who speaks against them is speaking against God. Yet the apostle Paul commended the people of Berea for searching the Scriptures to make sure he spoke the truth (Acts 17:10–11). Paul also stated to those in Galatia that if anyone, including himself, should teach another Gospel, that person should be accursed (Galatians 1:8–9). In everything, Paul kept directing people to Scripture as the final authority. Any men who claim to be apostles or prophets today often make themselves the final authority, something Paul and the Twelve never did.

18. **Read Acts 17:11, 1 Thessalonians 5:20–21, and 1 John 4:1. What do these verses instruct us to do?**

____

____

____

Church-Building Gifts

Today, the Lord uses the building gifts of evangelists and pastor-teachers to build upon the completed foundation, which was finished by the time Paul wrote Ephesians 2:20.

19. **Read Ephesians 2:19–22. Paul uses the images of a building project to describe the building of the Church. What is finished, and what continues to be built?**

____

____

____

Building on the Foundation

The Building Gifts Are Men

| 1. Evangelists | Proclaim the Gospel of Christ crucified to a dying world, whom God saves when they believe the evangelist's message. | Eph. 4:11 |
| 2. Pastor-Teachers | Build up in the faith those who are saved through the work of the evangelists. | Eph. 4:11–16 |

Unlike the foundation-building gifts, the church-building gifts continue to be appointed by the Lord, and affirmed within each local body, for the adding to and building up of the Body of Christ.

Evangelists

Ephesians 4:11 says, "And He Himself gave some to be . . . evangelists." Believers appointed to this position in the church have a unique,

God-given ability to win people to Christ. The only person in the New Testament who is labeled an evangelist is Philip in Acts 21:8. However, as with prophets who are not labeled prophets, can someone be an evangelist through observation of their evangelistic work? The answer is yes.

God's Word does not give us a lot of information about the building gift of evangelist. The person who holds this position is an overseer of his ministry and is affirmed by the results of people coming to know Christ. Philip is the only man named as an evangelist in the New Testament. He is known for his evangelistic ministry to the Ethiopian eunuch in Acts 9:25–40. The Apostle Peter saw three thousand souls saved on Pentecost as he exercised the gift of evangelism (Acts 2:14–42), and many more came to Christ in the weeks following. The Apostle Paul saw souls saved wherever he went on his missionary journeys. Therefore, we can conclude that the Apostles, including Paul, were evangelists as well as apostles and prophets. It is noteworthy that Timothy was told by Paul to do the work of an evangelist even though he was not titled in Scripture as an evangelist.

20. **Read 2 Timothy 4:5. If you do not have the gift of evangelist, what is your responsibility in this area?**

____

____

Pastor-Teachers

"And He Himself gave some to be . . . pastors and teachers" (Ephesians 4:11). A clearer translation of this is "the pastor-teacher." The definite article "the" appears before the word _pastors_ in the Greek text but not before _teachers_. This, combined with the conjunction "and" between pastor and teacher, makes them the same person with the multifaceted building gift of pastor-teacher. It is Jesus who calls or appoints to this office.

21. **Read Acts 20:28. Who is it that equips or enables them to carry out this appointment?**

____

____

Pastoring involves shepherding, which means guiding, leading, caring for, and feeding the flock. But a pastor will only be able to pastor the flock if he is able to teach them the Word of God. Everyone who has the gift of pastoring will have the gift of teaching because the two go together. The word for pastor and shepherd is the same Greek word, *poimen*.

22. **Read 1 Peter 5:1–4. What other words describe the pastor-teacher, and using your own words, what heart attitude should they display?**

____

____

There is a gift of teaching apart from pastor-teachers, but not everyone who has the gift of teaching will necessarily have the gift of pastoring. We will discuss this in book 2 of the Rooted and Grounded series.

Purposes of the Church-Building Gifts

Evangelists and those who do the work of an evangelist are often gifted as pastor-teachers, equippers, and builders of the church. The adage "catch a fish before you clean them" applies here. God saves a man or woman first; then He cleans them, changes them, equips them, and uses them.

23. **Read Ephesians 4:11–16. What are the three emphases of church builders (v.12)?**

____

____

24. **What are the four goals of the church builders (v. 13)?**

____

____

25. **Why are church builders supposed to grow mature believers from children to adults (v. 14)?**

____

____

26. **There are two inseparable ingredients that church builders are to use when building up the church. What are they (v. 15)?**

27. **What do verses 15 and 16 teach us about the importance of being in fellowship with other believers?**

Today, evangelists, pastor-teachers, and those doing the work of an evangelist are laying down the completed foundation throughout the world and building upon it.

28. **Read 1 Peter 2:4–6. What picture is given of the believers in relation to the cornerstone, Jesus Christ?**

Summary

The Apostles were prophets, and they were also evangelists and pastor-teachers. Jesus called and gifted twelve first-tier apostles and prophets. They are the finished foundation of the one Church, with Christ as the Chief Cornerstone. The building gifts were men chosen by Jesus to be evangelists and or pastor-teachers. Those gifts are men, and they continue until the Church is fully built.

Conclusion

We began this book by looking at our great salvation and then looked closely at the central figure of our salvation, Jesus Christ our Lord. Next, we examined our sin and why we need salvation that only God can provide. Understanding that Jesus is now sitting in heaven, we then looked closely at the person and works of the Holy Spirit, who carries out the work of saving mankind. After that, we focused on our Heavenly Father, who orchestrated our redemption by sending His eternal Son to die for us as the Son of Man. We then pulled together all three members of the Godhead and examined the Triunity, which works on our behalf. We then laid down the foundation of the Church, the Body of Christ, which will be explored in great detail in the next book.

1. **What should be our response to God for all that He has done for us? Write out your prayer of worship and thankfulness to our glorious God!**

____

____

____

____

____

Looking Ahead to Book Two

In Matthew 22:37–39, after Jesus was asked, "What is the greatest commandment in the law?" He responded, "'You shall love the LORD your God with all your heart, with all your soul, and with all your mind.' This is the first and great commandment. And the second is like it: 'You shall love your neighbor as yourself.'" Here, Jesus shows us two relationships, one toward God (vertical) and the other toward people (horizontal). You cannot truly love others until you first love God. This first book has focused on the vertical relationship with God—learning about His plan of redemption so that we can therefore have a right relationship with God, His Son Jesus Christ, and the Holy Spirit.

The next book will focus not only on our responsibilities toward God but also our relationships each other. We will be covering topics such as the trustworthiness of the Bible, the spirit world, Heaven and hell, the roles of Men and Women, Prayer, Worship, the Universal and local Church, and our interactions with the world.

www.ingramcontent.com/pod-product-compliance
Lightning Source LLC
Chambersburg PA
CBHW080358030726
47598CB00010B/2796